# Soul Lessons from the Wizard of Oz

*How to Follow <u>Your</u> Yellow Brick Road*

by Michael Shevack

© copyright 2019 Brains & Guts Entertainment, LLC

all rights reserved

No part of this publication may be reproduced, stored in a retrieval system or transmitted in any form or by any means, electronic, mechanical, photocopying, recording, scanning, or otherwise, except as permitted under Section 107 or 108 of the 1976 United States Copyright Act, without the prior written permission of the Publisher.

Limit of Liability/Disclaimer of Warranty: While the publisher and author have used their best efforts in preparing this book, they make no representations or warranties with respect to the accuracy or completeness of the contents of this book.

*Soul Lessons from the Wizard of Oz* is published and owned by Brains & Guts Entertainment, LLC.

Requests to the Publisher/Owner for permission should be sent to:

P.O. Box 655, Lahaska, PA 18931
Email: michael@michaelshevack.com

Quotes from *The Wizard of Oz* movie have been granted by the kind and generous permission of Warner Bros.

www.ozsoullessons.com

ISBN: 9781796300949

Brains & Guts Entertainment, LLC
PO Box 655
Lahaska, PA 18931

For Teddy and her Cairn terrier Isabella

With special thanks for the vision and encouragement of Alex Siegel, as well as Michael Coan, Charles-Duane-Boaz and Nancy-Channah Miller, and Scott Zakrewski.

Also, with thanks to: Tony Lamonte, book cover design and illustrations. And David Fisher, interior design and production.

And for our Wizard-therapists:
Dr. Evan Thomas and Dr. Frank DiBennardo.

## Introduction

Like millions of children, I used to scurry into the family room once a year to watch *The Wizard of Oz*.

The ritual began on a 50's style, primitive black and white T.V, so I couldn't witness the *Technicolor* miracle, as Dorothy threw open the door of her gray Kansas farmhouse and marveled at her first sight of Munchkin Land. Fortunately, a few years later, my Dad got us a color T.V. Like Dorothy, I too was amazed as an array of human flowers and side-show characters glided gracefully, like a living rainbow, before me.

Year after year, I stared transfixed as a Scarecrow, a Tin Man, a Cowardly Lion, and a young girl battled disgruntled apple trees, a vengeful witch, flying monkeys, and a poppy-laced field, in order to fulfill their heart's desires.

I soon learned the entire movie by heart. I could speak line after line, and often did so, in concert with the characters.

I could mimic the Mayor of the Munchkin City. I could vibrate my voice, eerily, like the Coroner Philosopher. Though never talented on my toes as a ballerina, I could easily dig my elbows into whomever was watching with me, like one of the roguish Lollipop Guild. As the *piece de resistance*, I could shriek like the Wicked Witch: *"I'll get you my pretty and your little dog too."*

The movie impressed itself upon my Soul, like a seal on melted wax. By the fourth grade I devoured the original book, shocked to find that Dorothy did not wear ruby slippers, but instead, silver slippers; the ruby slippers were the Hollywood screenwriter's suggestion. I was similarly shocked, but excited, to discover that in the book it wasn't a dream; Dorothy actually flew home from Oz, losing her slippers in the desert. "It wasn't a dream. It was real," I thought.

I *believed!* Oz was *real!*

A pivotal event in my Oz-obsession occurred when I was about eighteen, I came across an article, if I can remember correctly, in *Psychology Today*, on the psychological meaning of *The Wizard of Oz*. The author viewed the story as representing the relationship between a patient and his/her therapist. First, the patient sees the therapist as the "Wizard", called, in psychoanalytic language, *transference;* you project significant relationships, such as parental figures, upon the therapist to work out your early childhood problems.

Slowly, as patients follow their *Yellow Brick Road*, the course of therapy back to their True Selves, they come to realize that the power of the Wizard was really just an illusion. The therapist was not a Wizard after all, just an ordinary human being, with insight and compassion: *"Pay no attention to that man behind the curtain,"* said the fraudulent Wizard. The Power was not him. The Power was You!

For me at that time, terribly confused, and spending most of my money from a part-time job at the college library on therapy, it was comforting to know that, like Dorothy, I would eventually find my way out of the Witch's castle. *The Wizard of Oz* gave me faith to go through my own haunted forest. The Cowardly Lion was wrong – "*I do believe in spooks. I do… I do… I do believe in spooks,*" he fearfully repeated. One should *never* believe in spooks; it is believing in them that gives them power over you.

The article in *Psychology Today* was my first glimpse that under the simple, innocent grain of this story was a more profound meaning. My appetite whet, my Soul seemed to ache for an even deeper understanding of the story. I could sense that *The Wizard of Oz* was trying to tell me something. Besides a medal, a diploma and a ticking heart, the Wizard had something for me personally, something I needed in order to complete myself spiritually.

Looking back on it now, unbeknownst to me, at least the *conscious* me, my subconscious took up the task of deciphering the hidden message of the story. Over the next 15 years, I was totally unaware that some kind of understanding of the meaning of this story was gestating in the depths of my mind.

On a quest for the spiritual, since the age of 16, I did not realize that my understandings of Judaism, Christianity, Islam, Buddhism, *Kabbalah,* metaphysics, Hinduism and nature-religions, were weaving within me. Without my knowing it, the *archetypes*, as Carl Jung termed them, the mythic images of our *collective consciousness,* which seethe throughout the story of *The Wizard of Oz*, were organizing and transfiguring my thought processes.

Then, one day, lightning struck! Suddenly, in a blinding flash, like Moses confronting the burning bush, or St. Paul beholding the Risen Christ – though hardly on the same scale – the meaning of *The Wizard of Oz revealed itself* to me. I understood the message the Scarecrow had been trying to teach me all these years. I knew what the hollow rumbling of the Tin Man's chest was saying to me.

I understood the meaning of Dorothy's blue dress. The meaning of Kansas, the cyclone, the broomstick of the Witch, and the bucket of water that melted her. The story's inner meaning spread out before me like a spiritual smorgasbord. The characters became alive inside me! The book took on the air of scripture. Like a biblical verse, I could feel wave after wave of inspiration rippling towards me.

Consulting *The Annotated Wizard of Oz*, a huge compendium of Oz-related trivia, I was shocked to see that there was no mention of my revelation. Was L. Frank Baum unaware of his own subconscious and the meaning of his own characters? Or, "Perhaps, I'm just crazy?," I thought, and too busy with the dulling affairs of adult, Kansan life, I stuffed the Oz-vision back into my unconscious.

Some ten years later, at the age of 47, I was leaving New York's Port Authority Bus Station on route to a client and the vision suddenly surfaced, like a brainstorm in a brainless Scarecrow. "Write a book about the spiritual meaning of *The Wizard of Oz*," an inner voice commanded me. And, right then and there, I passed a gentleman leaning up against a girder, engrossed in *The Tao of Pooh*, a Zen Buddhist interpretation of that childhood tale. "If Pooh could offer safe passage to Nirvana," I thought, "certainly, *The Wizard of Oz* could?" It was a "sign".

Immediately afterwards, I received an e-mail from my buddy Chuck Kent, in which he made a playful reference to Dorothy to illustrate some point he was making. Strangely, I had never, ever mentioned my passion for the Wizard to Chuck. "Two signs," I exclaimed to myself, and with a fever near-evangelical, I jumped to the only scientific conclusion possible: "God wants me to write this." The world was calling this book out of me, for some reason.

And so here it is.

Dorothy's path back home is all our paths back home. But home is not in Kansas or any other geographical place. Home is in our heart. And so many of us have gotten caught in a whirlwind, when we ceased to follow *The Yellow Brick Road* of our own heart's desires. It was a lesson Dorothy struggled so very hard to understand. It's a spiritual lesson I struggled equally hard to understand and am only now just mastering. It's a struggle parents have. Children have. Everyone, in fact.

So, it's my sincere hope that with the help of this book you too might find your way home a lot easier, and that your children may not have to wander so far from their heart's desires to find their True Spiritual Selves.

After all, as Dorothy put it so poignantly, *"Oh, Auntie Em. There's no place like home."*

# Soul Lesson #1:

## Leave Kansas: The Ordinary State of Mind

It is *from* Kansas that Dorothy began her journey. It is *to* Kansas that Dorothy's journey lead. But, between the going and the coming, how Dorothy feels about Kansas, and its meaning for her, radically changes.

First, as Professor Marvel observed from his fraudulent crystal ball, Kansas is a place where no one understands her. It's a place where Dorothy cannot be herself, a threat to her own identity, and Toto's life. But after her journey to Oz, Kansas seems different to her. It is now the most perfect, most beautiful place of her heart's desire: home.

What has changed? Certainly not Kansas. It is as dull and gray as ever, with apologies to those in that fair state. No – it is not Kansas that's changed. It's Dorothy that has changed. She has changed her mind! She sees Kansas differently, and so it *is* different.

Changing your mind about how you see Life is what following your *Yellow Brick Road* is all about. First, you see something negatively; you are divided, hurt, alienated, confused, even desperate to escape. Afterwards, you begin to see the exact same situation from a positive vantagepoint: from a perspective of wholeness, of clarity, of pure love and forgiveness.

You begin to realize that you already had everything. You already had all the love, all the gifts, all the Powers of *Mind, Heart* and *Will* – your *Inner Scarecrow, Inner Tin Man* and *Inner Cowardly Lion* – but, you just didn't *realize* it!

Kansas is where all our spiritual journeys, no matter who you are or what you've experienced, start from. It is the prison of the ordinary. It admits no rainbows.

As children, we seem to have the innate ability to seize the world with openness of heart and see the world with bright-eyed wonder. Touching the leaves, feeling the sensation of our bare feet on the ground, smelling the odors wafting from the kitchen window, enjoying the wet nose of a puppy pressed against ours – these, for a child, are all *living* experiences.

They are fresh. They are new. They are experiences that the child has not yet learned to take for granted. As children, we live in a beautiful, colorful Munchkin Land, a place of pure freshness and imagination. A place of endless possibility and total delight. It's a world which seems to be made just for "little people".

But, soon, the joys of childhood fade. Adulthood presses against us, with greater and greater urgency. All sorts of expectations, largely imposed upon us by others, begin to encroach on our Spirit: "What do you want to do when you grow up?" "If you don't make enough money, you'll end up disadvantaged." "It's time you settled down." "When are you going to marry and have a family?" "Responsibility will mature you." They scream in your ear, like the menacing cackle of the Wicked Witch of the West.

The wonder of childhood is replaced by the worry of adulthood. Delightful, delicious, spontaneous behavior becomes replaced by robotic, routinized, ritualized, thoroughly adult, behavior. In truth, your life becomes *adult-erated*. Habit becomes the rule of life. Year after year, once the programming starts, the eyes of innocent children begin to dull and become glazed. We become hypnotized, mesmerized by the world and the world's beliefs about "rights" and "wrongs", "dos" and "don'ts". We become disconnected from the Light which is our Soul. From a colorful, imaginative Munchkin Land-of-possibility, our Spirits are reduced to a dull, gray, dusty, lifeless Kansas. The ordinary captures our Souls and imprisons it, like Dorothy in the Witch's castle.

Unfortunately, Kansas is how so many of us see our lives. Kansas is the realm of the ordinary. Kansas is what we see when we stop seeing miracles, and see just the surface, everyday, material reality. Kansas is what happens when we don't stop to "smell the roses" and appreciate the feel of sunlight on our backs, because "we are just too busy."

Kansas is the place of Auntie Em, or *Emily,* meaning *laboring*. Kansas is where we are lost in the work-a-day, scratching the ground for a living, so lost in the humdrum we are unable to look skyward and glimpse rainbows.

Kansas is what we experience, when we trust the fear-ridden expectations of the world over the Inner Light of our own Spiritual Being and Essence – born of the Creator, in whose *Image and Likeness* we are made.

Do you live in Kansas?

Kansas is in the "*mid*-west", that "gray area" between the cold, contraction of the east and the warm, expansion of the west. It represents a place lost in the middle without extremes, a boring place, without passion, without adventure, without wildness and excitement, ups and downs. It is Life purged of the thrills of extremes. It is Life "in the middle". No mountains to climb. No heavens to vault – and oh, so flat! A plain plane! So very sad.

Do you live in Kansas?

Like Dorothy, every Soul may be surrounded by loved ones, like Auntie Em or Uncle Henry, or friends like Zeke, Hunk or Hickory – but, we don't stop to realize how special these Souls are in our lives. We lose contact with the meaning of our closest relatives and companions, seldom giving them a thought of appreciation, more often considering them an annoyance or a burden.

Have you ever taken your spouse for granted? Have you forgotten why you fell in love with them?

Do you drive your car to work without appreciating the miracle of an automobile, or the blessing of actually having a job?

Do you spend your life just "hanging out" with friends, without challenging your mind, perhaps deadening your Spirit with too much T.V. or beer?

Has the burden of responsibilities, bills and more bills, over-shadowed your life? When was the last time you laughed worry-free?

In the story of *The Wizard of Oz*, Kansas is not just a state of America. It symbolizes a state of mind. Fortunately, it's a state of mind that can be changed. But first, you have to realize you're in Kansas in the first place.

The name *Dorothy* means *Gift of God*. We must all discover the Gift of God that is our very Soul.

We all need to leave Kansas, or we will remain spiritually dead.

# Soul Lesson #2:

## Believe in Rainbows: The Oz State of Mind

At first glance, for Dorothy, and for all of us, there is no escape from Kansas. We have been so conditioned to think of doing things in the "same old way". We are so programmed to believe that the routine we've established and have become entrenched in, is set in cement. We want to go *Somewhere Over the Rainbow*, but we don't know how.

But it is not Kansas itself that keeps us cemented where we are. It is our *belief* in the "power" of Kansas that does. It is the belief that "Life is just like that," "There's no other way," "This is just how it's done," that pins us to this spiritual wasteland. We believe that Kansas has some kind of power over us, and so it does. We are afraid to break away, and so we don't. We are afraid of staying where we are, because we're not happy. However, we're even more afraid of going *Somewhere Over the Rainbow,* because the unknown is fearful. Then, rather than confront our fear, we begin to rationalize that our dreams are impossible, so we cease to believe in anything but our own current unhappiness.

In order to go *Somewhere Over the Rainbow* – to a new place, a new land, filled with color, promise and possibility – you must turn away from the fear and your belief in the power of your fear. Even if the fear of the unknown or the fear of change (We all have that.) still grips you, you must not allow it to control you. You must let the fear go and go forward. You must believe in possibility, way beyond the fear, before you can leave the Kansas *Ordinary State of Mind*. You must have that great spiritual virtue called *faith*:

> *"Somewhere over the rainbow, way up high.*
> *There's a land that I heard of once in a lullaby."*

These words by the great lyricist Y.E. (Yip) Harburg, are not just part of a sentimental song, but a spiritual call-to-action.

They teach us one of the most important and powerful of spiritual principles: You must believe in something new, believe in a new possibility, a new adventure, a new approach to Life, before you accomplish it. Like an innocent child, you must believe in it, even if it seems as if there's only a whisper of possibility at the moment.

Even if your belief is only tiny and baby-like, still delicate, tender and fragile like the words of a lullaby, you must believe it with all your *Mind, Heart* and *Will* – your *Inner Scarecrow, Inner Tin Man, and Inner Cowardly Lion*. Like Dorothy, you must muster all the help of these inner companions, in order to begin the spiritual journey of making your dream come true.

> Ben always dreamed of leaving his father's business, which his father had inherited from his father; there was a lot of pressure to keep the tradition going. Ben didn't believe it was possible with a wife and children to support, and so he stayed where he was. His excuse ended with a painful separation, which made him aware of how his unhappiness had undermined his marriage.
>
> Forced to change, he believed in the possibility that this was an opportunity-in-disguise. Now he has his dream as a successful restaurant owner. He and his wife are reconciled.
>
> Rebecca was a single mother of three, living on welfare, with no way out. Until, one day, she got angry at her circumstances, swore that it was over, and she would find a better way. The next day, miraculously, she met a man who was looking for someone to work as an assistant in his real estate office.
>
> Explaining her circumstances, the man was very sympathetic, and was willing to help. It wasn't long before Rebecca had found her calling. She is now a real estate agent, and she and her three kids have a new home way far away from the urban sprawl.

To get out of Kansas, to get out of the *Ordinary State of Mind*, you've got to believe in rainbows. Once you do, you contact a powerful new state of mind, the *Oz State of Mind*. In this state of mind, all your "can't's" and "disbeliefs" which arise from your doubts, especially self-doubts, disappear. In the *Oz State of Mind*, your confusions between your Mind, Heart, and Will – your Inner Scarecrow, Inner Tin Man and Inner Cowardly Lion – dissolve. With these inner companions joined with you, arm-in-arm, you are no longer fighting yourself; all the previous energy you have been wasting in naysaying and negativity becomes focused into a single force of pure faith and positivity. This is the force of your *Spirit,* which we'll discuss in our next Soul Lesson.

Like Dorothy in the movie, once you open the door of your poor black and white Kansas farmhouse, to the Technicolor *Oz State of Mind*, you are *already* freed from the Kansas State of Mind. You have *already* freed your mind from the belief that you are stuck in a rut with no place to go. The moment you believe – truly believe – that there is a place *Somewhere Over the Rainbow,* you are already standing on the threshold to your spiritual and material freedom. You are already successful and have achieved your dream; your dream has already been planted in the universe. The rest is just the real-life adventure down your *Yellow Brick Road* towards your actual earthly harvest. There may be ups and downs, good witches and bad, but that's just grist-for-the-mill: *"The dreams that you dare to dream really do come true,"* once you believe in them.

Believe in a place *Somewhere Over the Rainbow.* Believe in a new Life, a new possibility, far away from Kansas. Access the *Oz State of Mind.* Discover the Power of faith. In the *Oz State of Mind*, miracles are everyday occurrences:

> *"If happy little bluebirds fly, beyond the rainbow,
> Why, Oh why, can't I?"*

No reason at all! Except you have failed to believe you can!

## Soul Lesson #3:

## Protect Toto: Your Precious Free Spirit

The moment you decide to change, the moment you decide to go *Somewhere Over the Rainbow*, problems start. Why? Because the other people who are still living in Kansas, who think it is an absolutely fine place to live, and who can't even imagine a rainbow, become intensely threatened.

They will call you a dreamer. They will try to make you believe that their "commonsense" way of doing things is the "right way". Guilt will be flung at you, and if you're not careful, it will stick to you like a fuzzball to *Velcro*. You will be made to feel that you are a betrayer, a self-indulgent "child", a selfish human being for wanting, like Dorothy, to journey beyond the corral of the farm.

They will attack you, because they're afraid of facing how you make them feel. You see, you are confronting them with themselves; your desire to have more out of

Life they take as criticism for their "lives of quiet desperation". By desiring to change, you force them to face their deep regrets, and they act out their jealousy of your declared freedom by condemning you.

In the story, this is symbolized by Dorothy's little pet, a feisty, dark-haired Cairn terrier named *Toto*. Toto is, true to his name, Dorothy's *totem animal*, as Native Americans describe it. Toto is the physical embodiment, in animal form, of Dorothy's *Free Spirit*.

Toto is not a perfectly well-behaved lap dog, with impeccable, white-gloved manners. Toto is free. He has no respect for authorities; he couldn't care less about someone who owns "half the county", like Elvira Gulch. He'll chase the cat in her garden, whether she likes it or not. He'll bite her leg just to show her his Spirit can't be squelched.

Toto represents the Free Spirit in all of us, which family, "friends", and society often force us to repress. Toto is our individual Spirit, which we are often coerced to forfeit in order to belong to the group, in order to be loved conditionally by others. And, there are a lot of conditions!

> Mom will love you, as long as you telephone her.
>
> The boss will love you, as long as you just shut up and just do what you're told.
>
> Your mate will love you, as long as you exhaust yourself and continue to bring home money.

Your religion, and their version of "God", will love you, as long as you repress yourself and fit into their belief system.

And sadly, because we all want to be loved – for it is the most basic of human spiritual needs – we often change ourselves and alter our dreams in order to win the love and approval of others. This gives others power over our Spirit. Our love for others, over ourselves, is what enslaves us!

The moment we decide to seek the *Oz State of Mind* and leave Kansas, the moment we decide we are not going to be like others, that there is something better beyond Kansas – the moment we decide to let out our Free Spirit and not keep our Light under a bushel, like Toto imprisoned in Elvira's bicycle basket – all hell breaks out. You are breaking the mold. You are destroying the unconscious patterns that people have lived by and held in place, unquestioningly, for generations.

*"That dog is a menace to the community,"* barked Elvira Gulch. *"I'm taking it to the Sheriff to be destroyed."* When you express your Toto-Spirit, your individuality can be seen as a threat to group-values, group-conditions, group-norms, and "group-think" in general.

Dorothy, like all of us, may live in Kansas bodily, but the Toto-in-us, our Spirit, is free of Kansas. Toto is a precious "animal", from the Latin *anima*, meaning *breath*. Within each of us, God has placed our "life-breath", our unique Spirit, God's Own Life Force in us. It is this that makes each of us an individual, a *Soul*.

So, when you sacrifice yourself for the conditional love of others, when you, like Dorothy, get stuck in the muck of the family pig sty rather than setting out *Somewhere Over the Rainbow* – you are not just betraying yourself or others, but more importantly, God, Who placed that Spirit inside you. To not follow the good, pure, free impulse of your God-given Spirit, because you prefer the love of others over the love of God, is to turn mere mortals into "gods". You become an *idolater*, to use the ancient religious term.

To a certain extent, idolatry is the normal state of childhood, where we see our parents and others as "bigger", i.e. more powerful than us, gods-of-sort. Dorothy sees Auntie Em, Uncle Henry, and Elvira Gulch this way, which is why she feels so controlled by them. We have all passed through this stage of psychological development.

However, in expressing our Spirit, in setting our Inner Toto free, in denying the power of others over it, we stop worshipping false gods. We declare our adulthood – not necessarily our physical adulthood with puberty and aging – but, our *spiritual adulthood.* We declare our own individuality and assert our Freedom-of-Spirit. We declare, as in the American *Declaration of Independence,* the Universal Truth that we are *"endowed by the Creator with certain inalienable rights"* of which no other human being has a right to deprive us, no matter how close to us, no matter how well-intentioned or loving:

Do you know any adults who never really declared their spiritual adulthood, and lived someone else's lives?

Do you know adults who, even upon their deathbed, had chosen to die spiritually, by sacrificing their dreams, long before their bodies gave in?

Don't let this happen to you! Dorothy didn't. Learn from her. Beware! Besides an *Inner Toto*, there is also an *Inner Elvira* or *Inner Witch* within each of us. Until she is melted, the Witch-in-us will constantly place doubt in our hearts, constantly try to repress our Spirit, imprison it, and destroy it. The Witch-in-us will constantly cackle all sorts of plausible, logical reasons or even menacing threats, why you should give up your dream to go *Somewhere Over the Rainbow*.

But fear not! Your Spirit is naturally strong. It is smart, indomitable, like Toto in the story. Your Spirit cannot be caged, contained, or controlled by anyone. Not even yourself! Toto escaped from Elvira's basket as a spiritual sign to us all; Spirit cannot be imprisoned!

Your Spirit is truly *Toto*, from the Latin, meaning *All:* It is All God-Power! It is all the Power your Oz-evolving Soul will need on the journey ahead.

On *The Yellow Brick Road* of your spiritual growth, never allow Toto to wander off. Always keep him at your side, a constant, truth-worthy companion. Protect your feisty, individualistic Spirit with every fiber of your being.

It will propel you *Somewhere Over the Rainbow*.

# Soul Lesson #4:

## Guilt: The Fake Professor

To tear away from loved ones, both relatives and friends, and set out *Somewhere Over the Rainbow*, can be a painful experience. You are not just leaving a dull, gray, Kansan life behind, you are also leaving warm, loving, human relations, people who care about you, people who – even if they have a narrow view of you – nevertheless, generally-speaking, nurtured you with a good heart.

Indeed, everyone's connection to their personal Kansas is very deep, emotionally and psychologically. Kansas is ingrained in you. It is your home. It is your culture, tradition, or way of life. The decision to express your Free Spirit, may not just threaten others, but also, a very real side of yourself. In a way, the people from whom you are separating, live inside you too; you can hear their thoughts and beliefs as your own from years of being around them. The decision to express your Free Spirit can feel like you are, in part, attacking yourself; it can force you to feel split, right down the middle, between the side of you that loves them, and the side of you that *must* love yourself. Many of us have experienced this kind of split; usually it surfaces as a life-altering event:

> Little Bill hits puberty and refuses to listen to his father, Big Bill, who does nothing but scream at him for being "a bum".
>
> A demure Dora looks in the mirror after 20 years of marriage and says, "I've turned into my mother," and suddenly lets out her True Self – to everyone's shock.
>
> Ted, from a straight-laced family, decides he's gay; he now "comes out", flamboyantly, while his previously-loving family condemns him, embarrassed.
>
> Becka, who dreamed of being a country western singer, but fell into bookkeeping to pay the bills, suddenly breaks all her pencils. Threatening family stability, she comes home with a cowgirl hat.

This is exactly what happens to Dorothy. She makes a radical break from the past in order to experience the dawn of spiritual freedom. In the movie we see Dorothy abruptly grabbing Toto, her Spirit. Clutching it tightly in her arms, so her ever-feisty Spirit won't get away, she packs her bag and tears away from home… in a huff. The anger is there to fuel her, so she can take that first and most difficult step… beyond the barnyard.

It isn't long though, before Dorothy, now a few miles from home, wanders into a campsite where Professor Marvel is cooking dinner over an open fire. Toto, acting the part of Dorothy's Free Spirit, lunges at a hot dog which the good "professor" is roasting. Symbolically, Dorothy's Spirit is hungering for some wisdom; she is feeling split and in pain. After making due apologies for Toto's impolite behavior, (Your Spirit can seem unruly once you let it out of the box.) Professor Marvel invites them both to dinner and the spiritual nourishment begins.

The Professor begins to tell Dorothy, who is dreaming of adventures beyond Kansas, all about the Crown Heads of Europe. But, as the viewer quickly learns, Professor Marvel (like the great Oz, played by the same actor) is a fraud, a quack, a carnival attraction, not at all the mystic or adventurer he pretends to be. After inviting Dorothy to close her eyes, so he can gaze into his crystal ball, he searches her pocketbook for some kind of clue about her. Coming across an old worn photograph, Professor Marvel now has all the information he needs to put on a false display of psychic prowess.

Faking a reverie, he tells a naïve Dorothy about the house he "sees", with a picket fence, and woman standing in front. Dorothy exclaims with amazement, *"That's Auntie Em,"* to which Marvel, displaying "con-clairvoyance", observes that *Em* stands for *Emily*. After that, with a dramatic flair that only a good con-man could muster, he goes on to say, *"She's crying. Someone has hurt her. Someone has just about broken her heart… What's this? She's putting her hand on her heart? She's dropping down on her bed."*

Marvel sized up the situation of poor Dorothy running away from home and drew upon her feelings of guilt to manipulate her to return home. Before you know it, cyclone brewing and all, Dorothy snatches her Toto-Spirit, and runs right back to the very Kansan life she was escaping. Her radical break to assert her Spirit has ended in a *false beginning.*

When we break from Kansas in our lives and decide, in faith, to seek *Somewhere Over the Rainbow,* we all need to be acutely aware of guilt *from* others or *over* others. Guilt is the great killer of your dreams. Guilt is the great destroyer of the *Oz State of Mind.* Guilt is how the people in Kansas stay in control of your Spirit!

By cutting off from the ways of the past abruptly, defying others around us, splitting ourselves painfully in two – we can easily fall into a chasm in which we blame ourselves for hurting others, or in which others blame us because they're feeling hurt. We can feel so much blame that we can generate a toxic level of guilt inside of us.

When it comes to guilt, it is very important to realize a very powerful spiritual truth: *You are not responsible for how anyone feels.* No matter what you do to another person, (unless you are intentionally evil or cruel,) how they feel is *their responsibility* not yours. Auntie Em's reaction to Dorothy's Spirit, is hers; she is responsible for it, not Dorothy.

Dorothy isn't hurting her; Auntie Em is feeling *her own hurt*, elicited through Dorothy – perhaps her own self-hatred for *laboring* (the meaning of *Emily)* her whole life in Kansas, when she wanted to be a cabaret star in Paris.

If others are threatened by your Spirit, and you feel guilty for abandoning their way, you are not doing anything wrong. If you feel guilt, when you break from the past to express your Spirit, this does not mean you are making a mistake and should not break from the past. Guilt is just one of many complex human emotions that we must pass through on our way to the *Oz State of Mind*.

Guilt is, like Professor Marvel, a fake professor. In the guise of teaching moral responsibility to the group, in the guise of reminding us of the important virtue of considering others and not merely ourselves, guilt creates self-hatred and spiritual martyrdom. Guilt coerces us to put others over ourselves just when, in order to break away from Kansas, we must muster the strength to put ourselves over others.

The guilt appears because the separation we are making is as yet immature, and we've not come to peace with the split in us, or the split between us and others. Our new Oz Self has not yet fully emerged from the womb; our true spiritual individuality is not fully anchored.

If there's a serious life-threatening situation, such as a severely ill child, putting yourself second is a moral responsibility. But, to sacrifice your God-given Spirit (allowing Elvira Gulch to capture it) so you don't upset the folks in Kansas, is a moral desecration of yourself. It dishonors the Light God placed inside you.

The best way to handle guilt, is to face it directly. Make an attempt to include others in your self-assertion. Continuing the examples above:

> "Hey Dad," said Little Bill. "I know I'm being a pain." "It's O.K. son," responded Big Bill. I went through puberty once myself."

> "Look, I know you've never seen me this way," said Dora. "But, I've been denying my True Self in order to appear like the 'perfect mother', and hating myself."

> "I know this is hard on you," assured a flamboyant Ted. "I will do everything possible to not embarrass you, but I must be myself."

> "Well," said Becka. "I know this is going to cause financial turmoil for a while, but I must try to follow my dream. Please help me through this."

You'll find that if you have *compassion* for yourself as well as for the people you may be upsetting, you won't feel as guilty, and they won't seem as angry. If you face your guilt, the guilt will generally lessen.

However, even if they don't budge, and they actually intensify their guilt-trip, (which they are free to do, and that's not your responsibility) as long as you know that you've given it "the ole' college try", you will be able to let them go, without feeling you've just walked out on responsibility and love to others. You'll leave Kansas with a clear conscience, so you will not, like Dorothy, run away, only to return – a false beginning.

But – warning – if you don't face your guilt, it can go *underground*. Like Auntie Em and Uncle Henry, guilt towards others can be driven into the storm cellar, your *subconscious*, locking you out. There, it can build force, unleashing a cyclone-of-emotion, a self-destructive force that can destroy your relationships and crash your hard-earned dreams in the future, when you least expect it.

Many a person who made a radical shift in their life and appeared to be doing so successfully – at least for a while – has found themselves crashed, years later, when the cyclone-of-guilt resurfaced from the storm cellar and wreaked havoc.

Face your guilt and you'll befriend it. Ignore your guilt, and you'll see the future through a fake crystal ball that predicts doom.

# Soul Lesson #5:

# Find the Center of Your Cyclone.

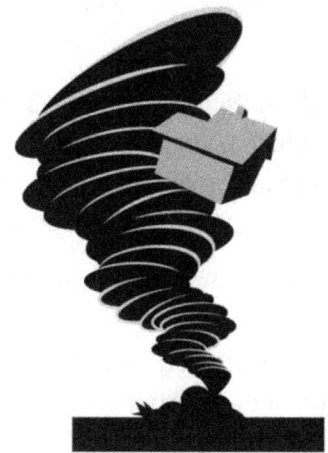

Sadly, Dorothy did not have the opportunity to confront her guilt. Just as Dorothy arrived back at the farm the objects of her guilt, Auntie Em and Uncle Henry, went into the storm cellar. Her emotions were now driven underground into Dorothy's subconscious mind. They would symbolically surface in the story as the whirling cyclone.

Our freedom-seeking Dorothy is torn between family and self, between Kansas and Oz, between self-expression and loyalty to others. Her feelings are whirling out-of-control, expressing themselves conceptually – as conflicting feelings usually do – in the form of "opposites" in our mind:

>me *vs.* them
>family control *vs.* individual freedom

> safety of home *vs.* fear of unknown
> pig sties *vs.* adventure

In the minds around us, in the society that surrounds us, there are many opposites. They can be very complex, even political:

> male freedom *vs.* female independence
> advancing technology *vs.* ecological safety
> government authority *vs.* self-expression
> higher interest *vs.* higher real estate prices

Whether you realize it or not, we all see Life through some kind of polarized lens. Unfortunately, when we make a decision based on such a polarized view, we experience a polarized life. The whirling opposites in our minds create a devastating cyclone around us:

> Sue wants to be out in the world working but was raised to think she's abandoning her children by doing so. She is constantly guilt-ridden and defending herself. Where did her mother learn to teach the opposite "working mom" *vs.* "real mom"?

> Mendy is prone to frequent displays of anger at people in charge, like bosses, because he was raised by an overbearing father. Where did his father learn the opposite "respect for authority" *vs.* "individual-expression"?

> Farmers in the north began to burn crops to keep the prices up, inspite of the fact that there are hungry people. How did the economic system become founded on the opposite "scarcity" *vs.* "low prices"?

In our individual mind, in the minds of the group, in the mind of society, our schools, our government, our social systems, our sciences – in all human thinking, all over the world – we, like Dorothy, are constantly bombarded, and are constantly bombarding ourselves and each other, with the opposites that whirl inside us.

What are these opposites? They are usually some kind of "black" *vs.* "white" value judgements, some "right" *vs.* "wrong", some kind of heart-bias or prejudice. In general, our inner opposites are usually a belief – some "this" *vs.* "that" – which our heart believes is true because, at one time in our lives, we experienced it to be so and learned accordingly.

Or, our inner opposites may be such a deep, ingrained belief, part of the general human experience, that they are actually believed to be set in cement and unavoidable: poverty, debilitated old ages, taxes, are some of the more cemented polarized beliefs. We actually consider these beliefs to be so real, we think they're part of being "realistic".

Wherever they arise from, once the polarized belief becomes accepted by your heart, it becomes entrenched in your psyche and, as Jesus put it so succinctly, *"It is accorded to you as you believe."* Our beliefs are like "computer programs" that control our thinking and doing, determining the life we are experiencing in the flesh.

Our beliefs program what we are sowing and reaping in Life. Each belief is delivered, like a prayer, into the depths of our consciousness, where it connects to the Consciousness behind all existence, God. Here, our beliefs become energized and enter into the "divine dream machine" which manufactures our shared experiences of reality. We often don't realize we are doing this, or that our beliefs, like prayers, are constantly being answered, weaving the fabric of our real-life experience. But they are!

As people, we are continuously believing things to be a certain way, and therefore, desiring them a certain way and creating them in our experience a certain way. The only difference between a Kansan and someone with the *Oz State of Mind*, is that the latter *knows* they are doing it and chooses their beliefs more consciously, cautiously, and carefully.

Indeed, it is because we are constantly seeding our reality with our beliefs, that any event in our life can be viewed in reverse, as a lesson. We can backtrack any negative (or positive) experience to the beliefs that created it, thereby learning about ourselves. In this way, we can learn a lot about our polarized lenses. This is how we discover a "mistake".

When we begin to free ourselves from the cyclone-of-opposites, from all the heart-believed beliefs that are adversely programming our life experiences, we take the first step to achieving the *Oz State of Mind*. How can we do it? Let's follow Dorothy's example in the movie:

> Knowing that you have surrounded your life with whirling opposites which are causing you difficulties – take a moment, inspite of the turbulent winds – to sit quietly on your bed.

Close your eyes. Don't fight the whirling opposites in you. Don't fight the conflicting thoughts. This will only make the turbulent winds stronger. Instead, sit back like Dorothy in the movie. Try to watch the thoughts your mind is producing, like an objective observer viewing yourself.

Like Dorothy, you may notice all sorts of whirling opposites and emotionally-laden thoughts. You may see Hunk, Zeke, Hickory, scenes from the past, barnyard animals, even your greatest fears like Elvira Gulch or the Wicked Witch. You'll notice your mind divided into "good witches" and "bad witches", rights and wrongs you seem to take for granted automatically. Try to watch them like Dorothy, unemotionally, letting them fly by.

Or, let them continue to fly by, until you feel totally unemotional about them and they seem like mere phenomena, like something unreal.

If you continue doing this exercise, something amazing will begin to happen, as it did for our heroine. Soon, in this *meditation* – for that's what it is – you will become detached from your problems. You will begin to sit by like Dorothy, calmly watching them, impartially, curiously, and calmly as they fly by, waving whimsically to you. Your mind and the wizardry of its "movie projector" becomes detached from your emotional pain or subconscious guilt. Soon, your mind will not sustain your whirling opposites anymore.

Then, something miraculous happens. Underneath the whirlwind, you will begin to notice something else, something very peaceful, very quiet. It will feel like an opening, a doorway into the depths of your being.

This is your True Center, the core Spiritual Self, which lies within every individual. This Spiritual Center, which exists within all of us, is the *Still Small Voice* of God of which the Bible speaks. It is the *Zen Mind*, or *Christ Consciousness*: You are aware of *being conscious* and that just being conscious connects you to a *Conscious Being* far greater than yourself. This Being, the more you commune with it, begins to feel like Pure Love and Infinite Possibility – the Loving Nature of God.

And, as you go deeper into the Center of your Cyclone, your consciousness spiraling higher and higher, past the storm clouds, past the whirling winds, past the worries, phobias, roles, and societal expectations, soon – emerging from the depths of your Inner God Self – you will begin to experience new thoughts, new visions and never-before-imagined possibilities.

You start thinking with the *Oz State of Mind*. You are no longer just idly dreaming of going *Somewhere Over the Rainbow*, partially disbelieving its possibility. You are now envisioning going *Somewhere Over the Rainbow* with crystal clarity, with the complete certainty of love and pure faith.

Projecting it with *Technicolor*-imagination upon the movie screen of your mind, lovingly embracing it by your heart, you send your desire to the depths of that Being Who lies also within you.

Now instead of seeding whirling opposites, you realize you have the Power to seed calm winds and beautiful, tranquil thoughts and dreams, instead.

This is the Spiritual Power that lies at the Center of your Cyclone. Get to know it!

Dissolve all your opposites into that Place – as the song goes – *"where troubles melt like lemon drops, away above the chimney tops. That's where you'll find ME,"* i.e. your True Self, God's Own Spirit Within.

This is the *Oz State of Mind*. This is Pure Divine Creativity which, combined with the feeling of Pure Love and Goodness, is your Complete Human Nature.

With great thanks and love to my teacher, the late Dr. John Lilly, M.D. whose work, *Center of the Cyclone*, changed my life. Thanks, and love also to Lee and Glen of the Samadhi Tank Co. in Nevada City, who tirelessly continue Dr. Lilly's work.

*Soul Lesson # 6:*

*Release the Power of your Inner Munchkin.*

Bump! Dorothy's farmhouse lands with a thud. Lifting herself off the mattress, cautiously walking out of the door – with what is perhaps the greatest understatement in movie history – Dorothy observes, *"Toto. I have a feeling we're not in Kansas anymore."*

Dorothy has arrived *Somewhere Over the Rainbow*. She is in a land *"way up high"*. She has ascended to Oz. She has forged the connection to her God Self. She's begun to discover the Inner Light which is her *Soul*.

Now, one might think, based on the previous Oz Soul Lesson, that this can only be accomplished by surviving a cyclone. You might think connecting to your *Oz State of Mind* requires braving tormenting winds, shattered windows, and emotional or physical pain. Sadly, many religions in the past have taught that spiritual awakening requires such suffering.

However, opening up the connection to the *Oz State of Mind,* does not require anything so self-punitive. All you really need is to joyfully express the pure, innocent *Inner Child* within you.

Your Inner Child is the natural expression of the pure, unsullied, God Self you were born with, before the Kansans began conditioning you and turning your rainbow gray. Indeed, every Soul, every Dorothy, needs to shed this *adult-eration* of our Inner Child and arrive in Munchkin Land, where we can re-access the enormous Spiritual Power of the "little person" inside us.

Our Inner Munchkin lives – no, not just lives, but thrives – through the Power of Pure Imagination. As children, we play "house", "cowboys and Native-Americans". We may, as in the movie, dream to be a ballerina in the Lullaby League or a rogue in the Lollipop Guild.

Our Inner Munchkin is filled with excitement for Life. Our Inner Munchkin is bright-eyed, brazen, defiant, tender, brash – part flower, part Coroner Philosopher, part Mayor – a strange combination of thoughts, feelings and "little characters" that live inside us.

Our Inner Munchkin can't resist trying this and trying that, experimenting with every sensation of this world, expressing the pure delight of wide-eyed childhood. For this reason, our Inner Munchkin never has a faith crisis. It never has difficulty believing that dreams can become reality. It naturally expresses the *Oz State of Mind.* Our Inner Munchkin, because it approaches Life with an unopposed mind and purity-of-heart, naturally understands faith, without needing any religious indoctrination, boring sermons, or books like this. Our Inner Munchkin can see with the Pure Power of our Soul-Vision.

Like every Dorothy, we all have a Soul-Vision. From the moment we are born, if you were around wise people who were trained to see it, there are very strong indications of what your Soul-Vision is, and what your true spiritual nature and earthly contribution should be. Your Soul-Vision is "hard wired" into you. It begins to express itself the instant you pop out of the womb, and, in fact, before.

Sadly, in today's spiritually empty world, where there are billions of bytes of information but very little wisdom, you might not be able to find a guide for your Soul-Vision. Like Dorothy – or myself – you might have to "hunt and peck", allowing Life to be your guide. That can be hard if you never learned to trust yourself, or worse, learned to trust others over your own Soul-Vision.

However, finding your Soul-Vision can be easy, and Life can be quite an excellent Soul-Guide, if you permit your Inner Munchkin to just express itself naturally, through the most common of child-like activities — no less a part of adulthood — *play*:

> At 6 years old, Christian was breaking old toys apart and re-assembling the pieces with tape into new toys? What do you think his Soul-Vision is?

At the age of 18 months, Adam discovered screwdrivers, and took the handle off the dishwasher. What do you think his Soul-Vision is?

At the age of 3, Zoe could memorize the lines from songs or movies, only hearing or seeing them once. What do you think her Soul-Vision is?

These are our kids, and my wife Teddy and I are still waiting to see their completed Soul-Vision. But, within each of our little Munchkins, we could easily see the vision inscribed within their Souls, expressing itself through natural play, natural talents, natural likes and dislikes, weaving their lives right in front of our eyes.

Whether you are a "real child" or a fully grown "adult child", is irrelevant. Within you is the Power of your Inner Child – the pure imagination and natural self-expression of a Munchkin, if not an entire city of Munchkins. You have talent upon talent, ability upon ability, which, if you set them free to develop through play, will gradually weave your Soul-Vision and earthly destiny.

If you ever get lost in Life, lost in a job you cannot stand, forget who you are, and are in need of expert guidance for direction on "what to do", just look to your Inner Munchkin. Ask yourself, "What games do I love to play? What are my fantasies?" Ask yourself, even at the age of 60 or more, "What do I want to be when I grow up?" And then, *grow!* Never stop being a child!

It is through accessing your Inner Munchkin, allowing yourself the freedom, at any age, to play, explore, test new waters, try new approaches, seek new adventures – that you open the door to the unabashed creative expression which is characteristic of the *Oz State of Mind.*

Your Inner Munchkin is effortlessly creative. It doesn't have to struggle. It doesn't have to strain like Kansan adults. Idea after idea just flows naturally like a stream. Connecting to your Inner Munchkin, you banish the humdrum. Even if you are born in modest circumstances, your imagination can turn a simple sandbox into an empire. Indeed, you can eventually create a real-life empire from the lessons gleaned in your sandbox.

Through the Soul-Vision of your Inner Munchkin, you will see Life and everything it has to offer through what Zen Buddhists call *The Beginner Mind.* With such a mind, even the most "ordinary" everyday experiences seem extraordinary. The simplest, "most common" things appear wondrous – a flower growing, a bird singing, the motion of your chest, as you inhale and exhale.

How do you access the Beginner Mind of your Inner Munchkin? Follow these few basic guidelines; they're especially important before setting out, like Dorothy, on your Soul's *Yellow Brick Road:*

> **Shed the trappings of ego.** Ego – a sense of your own "I"-ness – is a wonderful gift; we wouldn't be human without it. But, when the ego becomes a tyrant, measuring your thoughts, behaviors, and actions as well as

those of others, you bind and gag your Inner Munchkin. Try to stay clear of "adult-erated" thinking. Set yourself and others free.

**Be thoroughly willing to risk the possibility that you will look ridiculous.** No child would fantasize and play act, if they worried about how they appeared. Let go of your concern about how other people see you.

This requires bravery. Be brave as a child!

**Don't worry, at first, about practicalities.** Let yourself play with new ideas, new behaviors but don't worry about what you're "going to do" with them. If you want to play sports, then play sports. If you want to write, write. Just let out your natural play and give it the freedom to lead you. Don't lead it!

**Never fear fear.** There are fears that help you, like the fear that protects you by stopping you from jumping off a building; obey that kind of fear. But, never respect the fear that comes from programmed-Kansan thinking from the past. Don't give it any power or attention. Don't feed it. In fact, drain it of control over you by ignoring it, completely.

If you follow these basic guidelines, your Soul, your Inner Dorothy, will arrive in Munchkin Land and access the Pure Power of your Inner Munchkin with song, dance and trilling voices. You will reconnect easily, naturally, and playfully with the innocent, purely loving, child-like expression of your God Self, no matter what your age.

Then, the "little talents", "odd characters", and the entire city of Munchkins inside you, will celebrate your achievement:

> "Ding. Dong. The Witch is Dead.
> Witch Ole' Witch? The Wicked Witch."

You will have "killed the Witch" inside you. You will have dropped your Kansas farmhouse on your Inner Witch, stopping her from imprisoning your Inner Child. You will have killed that controlling, programmed, Kansan side of yourself that wants to keep you from discovering the spiritual secret of the ages:

> You are a Child-of-God.
> The whole world is your sandbox.

You are the shaper of your dreams. You are Freedom in human form. And, the only restriction is that you have to play nice. This most basic lesson of childhood is also the most powerful spiritual lesson for adults.

As Glinda sang to all the Munchkins:

> "We bring you good things. Or, haven't you heard?
> When she fell out of Kansas a miracle occurred."

All the miracles in your life – for Life itself is all miracle – begin with the discovery of your Inner Munchkin. Munchkin Land is not a fantasy. It is everyday reality – Kansas-transfigured — once you let your Inner Child play and find its way.

## Soul Lesson #7

## Learn from your Inner Witches.

*"O Rubbish. Begone. You have no power here in Munchkin Land,"* trilled Glinda the Good to the Wicked Witch of the West. Those who've reconnected to their Inner Munchkin and have raised their consciousness to the *Oz State of Mind*, have witnessed the Truth of Glinda's assertion firsthand.

Connecting to your Inner Child with an open, innocent heart, and a clear, undivided mind, changes your experience of Life. You no longer feel like a victim of a chaotic, frenzied, witch-ridden or evil world. Instead, you begin to experience Life as it is actually is: A beautifully ordered, living state of Grace, Providence, Divine Protection or Guidance. You begin to notice that everything begins to go more smoothly, with an astonishing choreography to the events:

You may think something, and suddenly the phone will ring. You may need something, and just as you do, you will pass it on the street. Your inner life and your outer life increasingly mirror each other. As the song goes, *"troubles melt like lemon drops."* You and everyone around you begin to feel like "one body".

If you are a devout Christian, you might call this experience being *born again* – which, in the original Greek also means *begotten from above*. Ascending from Kansas to Oz, asserting your Power as a Child-of-God, you are reborn into a higher *Oz State of Mind*. Life becomes transformed, a common spiritual experience reported by all the world's great faiths.

The more you experience this Divine Grace, the more you will not fear the Wicked Witch of the West when she flames onto the scene with her demonic cackle: *"I'll get you my pretty and your little dog too."* However, until you anchor the *Oz State of Mind* and it becomes your permanent state of consciousness, the Witch of the West is someone with whom you must contend.

To set ourselves free from Kansas, we first dropped a house on the Wicked Witch of the East; she's the *Witch-of-contraction*, like the cold, constricted, east coast. She's the Witch that narrowed all your options, getting you stuck in the mud of a Kansas pig sty.

However, the Wicked Witch of the West is considerably more menacing; as Glinda remarks to Dorothy, *"I'm afraid she's worse than the other one was."* The "west" is fierce, wildly-open, even reckless, like the rocky, twisting west coast. This is the Inner Witch that terrifies us most. The Witch-of-contraction can, on some level, make us feel "safe" in the routine, ordinary

Kansan world. But, the *Witch-of-expansion* takes no prisoners!

The Witch of the West represents our fear of our unlimited freedom and power, the fear of God's-Own-Light within. This Light terrifies us, because it forces us to expand, to express, to become more than we believe we are.

The Light forces us to face ourselves as mortals. It forces us to face how small we have been living. It forces us to face that we've wasted years of our life believing in Kansas instead of Oz. It forces us to confront our own potential and the difficult moral issues surrounding the use of human power.

The Witch of the West preys upon our fear of becoming too strong. The Witch of the West preys also upon our neurotic habit of making ourselves weak in order to attract Light from others, rather than discover and release our own.

The Witch of the West taunts us, making us afraid of our Light, afraid that if we express it, we may disconnect from loved ones completely and may never get back to Kansas; that's her hold over Dorothy throughout the story. The Witch will do everything within her wicked power to prevent us from experiencing the freedom of our Inner Light. She does not want us to discover our spiritual power. She eats our Inner Child.

The Witch of the West is ugly because she reflects the ugliest side of ourselves – the side that hides from our Inner Light and then blames the "wicked" people in the world who have "prevented us" from achieving our happiness and success. In reality, it is we who permitted them to stop us, because, tainted by the Witch of the West, it is we who were afraid of the Light of our own Power.

The Witch is sickeningly green-faced because she reflects the *envy* inside of us. Everyone who has failed to express their Inner Light carries a deep bitterness within them. They often resent others who "have more" at the same time as they condemn them for achieving it. They find ways to blame others for their own fear of expansion, including levying sizeable moral or religious indictments against them. The green-of-envy, when it is turned into a powerful, positive, proactive, spiritual-ascent – Light Released! – is transmuted into the Power of *emeralds*, which we'll talk about later.

One way to defeat the Witch of the West is to get clear about your fear of expansion. Just because you feel fear doesn't mean that it *is* fear. If you've ever gone on a roller-coaster and felt fear, you will notice that this fear is really *excitement-resisted*. You are terribly excited about the twists and turns of the ride, but you resist the excitement – hold back from it – and that is what produces the sense of fear. Holding back the excitement of your Inner Light can feel like a witch, when it is really an angel in a Halloween mask.

Instead of resisting the excitement of expansion, try throwing yourself into the delight of the Witch's terror. If you get into the spirit and fun of facing your fear of expansion, it will energize you rather than deplete you. If you positively embrace your Witch as a teacher, or even a friend – someone reflecting an aspect of your own psyche so you can learn more about yourself – you'll bend her power to fuel your expansion rather than hinder it. You'll take away her ugliness, and can actually learn to see the Witch as quite a lovely lady, green skin and all:

> Bob was terrified of facing his wife and asking her for a divorce, inspite of the fact that she was abusive. His Inner Wicked Witch of the West was always cackling, "You'll never find someone else. No one can love you."
>
> Instead of giving credence to his fears of expansion, Bob began to recognize that his Inner Witch of the West was a reflection of his own low self-esteem. He started to learn from her rather than fear her. After some counseling, he realized that there was a lot to love about himself. He divorced, re-married, and is now enjoying expansion with no fear. *"Ding. Dong. The Witch is dead."*

By paying attention to the "buttons" that your Inner Witch of the West pushes in you, you can learn a tremendous amount about yourself, which will help free your expansion into Oz consciousness. The more you realize the Witch's power over you comes from your fears, the more you will also realize you are the one in control, not her. Control your fears and the Witch can't harm you.

But, the best way to defeat the Witch of the West, is to not fight the Witch-in-you; that only forfeits your energy to the Witch and makes her grow more terrifying, as she feeds off your efforts to control her. Like all phobias of expansion, such as "fear of flying", the more you obsess over it, the worse it gets.

Instead, allow a beautiful bubble of inspiration to descend into Munchkin Land: A clear, lucid, brilliantly-reflective Light to help keep the Witch at bay and keep you anchored in the newly-found Grace of your Inner Child-Munchkin. At the first sign of the Witch of the West, call upon your *Inner Glinda*!

Glinda, the Witch of the North, is a good witch. She is like the archetype of a Fairy God Mother. She represents our Spirit Guide, that helpful being or beings that guide us on our journey. We all have one, or more, and if we call upon them, and trust the message that comes through our thoughts and feelings, they can be great allies.

Glinda is from the North, the perfect, always-reliable, magnetic-north of a compass. Glinda is a reminder that deep within us, there is a built-in compass-heading, that points us home to our True Selves – the Center of our Cyclone, the Inner Silence and Presence of God-Within. When the Witch shows her ugly face, if you allow your Glinda-compass to direct your attention inward, while listening deeply to your Inner Self – you will begin to hear your *Still Small Voice* bubbling up with friendly, lucid counsel.

New inspired ideas will once again enter your brain. Hitherto unthought-of approaches for dealing with wicked life circumstances will surface. Consult your Glinda-compass, and you'll move away from the Witch's ugliness toward the beautiful direction of the Light-within-you. The Wicked Ole' Witch – all your fears of expansion, all your fears of the enormous Light within you – will begin melt away into the Being of your True Self.

That's why, no matter how many times the Wicked Witch menaces you or threatens the death of you and your Toto-Spirit, she can never win. She is already defeated by your Inner Glinda, who will constantly, as all Spirit Guides do, point the way to a Power far greater than anything in Oz, including the Wizard: God's Own Power within you.

Enjoy your newly-found Grace in Munchkin Land. Have no fear!

For every pointed hat, there is a round bubble of inspiration. For every craggy cackle, there is a sweet, mellifluous voice. For every flying broomstick, there is a magic wand.

> For every witch that threatens, there is a Glinda who will always be there to protect you.

# Soul Lesson #8:

## Moral Balance:
## Stay in your Ruby Slippers.

The Wicked Witch of the West and Glinda the Good represent another critical Soul Lesson. They are symbols of a battle which often rages in all of us, as well as in the world: The battle between evil and good, between devils and angels, between "sons of darkness" and "sons of light", *Gog* and *Magog,* Satan and God; virtually every major world religion has its own version of the Wicked Witch of the West and Glinda the Good. On our spiritual path, we are all confronted with this moral battle.

Generally-speaking, as long as you face the issue of good *vs.* evil from the standpoint of simple moral choice, you can handle it fairly easily. There's simply "right" *vs.* "wrong", "proper" *vs.* "improper". For the most part, many of the rules and regulations we have learned as to what is right and wrong have a solid, obvious, basis in God. If you murder someone, they suffer, and that is not *Good*, i.e. from *God*; if you steal, you violate another person, and that is not Good i.e. from God.

However, when we begin to look at Life from the *Oz State of Mind*, from a unified, spiritual perspective, the issue of good *vs.* evil is no longer as simple or as childlike as a pretty Glinda *vs.* an ugly Witch. As we've seen in the last Soul Lesson, the ugly, green Wicked Witch of the West is not some mere wanton, immoral creature that must be destroyed, annihilated, wiped off the face of the earth with religious fervor. She can also be seen as a symbol of our own selves mirrored back to us:

It is *we* who have a scathing, judgmental witch inside of us. It is we who have a side of us that is hateful, vicious, and wants to destroy goodness. It is we that care only about ourselves and our own freedom and self-expression, so much so, we hurt Auntie Em and forsake the goodness we were raised with. We all have a Witch-side inside us. The real-life witches that enter our lives are, in a way, a reflection of that; we mirror who we, in part, are.

Besides, let us look squarely at Glinda the Good. Just because she is so beautiful, so pure, so lily-white (with apologies to peoples of "color") doesn't mean that these qualities are always so good. Such passive, cliché, feminine goodness has led to great victimization of women, so much so that a feminist revolution had to be created to free women from it. Indeed, wasn't Dorothy's pure goodness – so pretty, so perfect, so Glinda-like – partly responsible for the fact that no one in Kansas took her dreams seriously? Wasn't that the reason they brushed her aside, treated her like a mere female-child, ignoring and imprisoning her Toto-Spirit in Elvira's bike-basket?

As Glinda asked Dorothy, when she first arrived in Oz, *"Are you a good witch or a bad witch?"* Sometimes the distinctions between good and evil are not very clear but get terrifyingly blurred in certain situations. For instance, a cruel, demagogue of a Hitler can be considered a savior by a humiliated people after World War I; or, someone considered a savior, exemplifying peace and love, can be crucified. Excessive goodness can appear evil because your Soul's Light can feel threatened when you resist spiritual expansion; that's the Witch-of-expansion, the Witch of the West.

On the other hand, excessive evil can also appear good. Excessive evil often de-stabilizes habit-entrenched situations that are obstructing our spiritual evolution and need to be dislodged. Excessive evil can plunge us out of our comfort zone, forcing us to grow. Excessive evil can expose an evil that was percolating underneath our previous stage of good, re-empowering our ascent to Oz. Indeed, even a very good, political revolution – like the American – has a titch of evil in it.

Like all the opposites of human mental judgements, these opposites whirl in the cyclone of our minds. They whirl because the lines between them are not concrete. The moment we soften the lines, beyond the strict Kansan moral stereotypes, it's not easy to know, based on mere mental judgements alone, who's the Good Witch and who's the Bad Witch:

Mitch is in a job climbing the corporate ladder. Part of his job is to beat his competitors. Is he a good witch – an excellent breadwinner? Or, is he a bad witch – a human being with a business goal to hurt others?

Terry comes from a long line of poverty-stricken people. Determined to break the chain, she pushes her children for success and more success. Is she a good witch – helping to free her children? Or, is she a bad witch – putting her kids under excessive stress to accomplish monetarily?

Certainly, when in doubt, it's always good to follow your Inner Glinda-compass and "check in" with a Higher Power, seeking inner counsel. However, how can we be sure that the advice we get is good? As the expression goes, "the road to hell is paved with good intentions." Many a psychotic murderer or deranged cult-leader has "checked in" and come out with advice "directly from God" that leads to evil, in perhaps its purest, most knowable form.

Once we are firmly established in the *Oz State of Mind*, guided by God's Grace, the issue of *good vs. evil* will cease to be a tedious, tiresome mental debate. It will become transformed by a natural, shared, spiritually-aligned, living understanding between ourselves, humankind, and all Life and Creation.

But until this *Oz State of Mind* is anchored, we Kansans have a desperate need for some kind of basic, intellectual "helper" to keep us from falling into the crack between good and evil.

The key is *balance*. The greatest spiritual teachers in the world advise all Dorothy-Souls on the path of Oz, to not be swayed by appearances, to not judge by simple, outward appearances whether someone is a Good Witch or a Bad Witch. Instead, they advise seeking an authentic balance, weighing the goods and evils in any situation, trying hard to never favor one polarity excessively over another:

> Strictness should be balanced with compassion. Moral responsibility should be balanced with individual freedom.
>
> Passion should be balanced with sensibility. Law should be balanced with love. Enthusiasm should be balanced with caution.
>
> Inflation should be balanced with recession. Aid to the poor should be balanced with aid to self-reliance.
>
> Expenditures should be balanced with savings. And, in general, blacks and whites should be balanced with plenty of different shades of gray.

Balance, when you think about it, is the best solution to virtually all our current moral crises, personal or national – unless we want to live unbalanced, caught in the polarities of over-policing *vs.* wanton chaos.

However, there is also a "dangerous balance" that can be caused by strict, law-based, contracted, controlling Kansan life. This so-called "balance", contaminated by fear and ego, is artificial. It is rigid. It is not natural. It does not flow with Life. It needs to shift poles to a more spiritual balance, or, it will endanger the advancement of our Souls.

That's why, as soon as Glinda becomes aware of the threat to Dorothy by the Wicked Witch of the West, she transfers the ruby slippers from the feet of the Witch of the East to Dorothy. Despite the fact that the Witch of the West tries to badger Dorothy, *"Give me back my slippers. I'm the only one who knows how to use their power. They're no use to you. Give them back to me. Give them back,"* Glinda cautions Dorothy emphatically:

> *"Stay tight inside them. Their magic must be very powerful, or she wouldn't want them that badly."*

Dorothy will need balance more than ever, in her torturous Oz-expansion ahead.

As experts in crystals will tell you, rubies embody the spiritual power associated with balance, including flexibility, confidence, energy, vitality, leadership and emotion. Ruby-red is the color of our Light Body at our *sacrum* – from the same Latin root meaning *sacred* – the foundation of our spinal cord, where God's Light first roots itself into the physical upon birth. Corresponding to the *first chakra* of Hindu metaphysical systems or the blood of Christ's passion, ruby-red is the color of deep, perfectly-balanced safety in relationship to Life on earth.

By placing the ruby slippers on Dorothy's feet, Glinda is supplying Dorothy, and all of us, with a powerful Soul Lesson: *Stay balanced. Seek balance. Never lose your balance.* Avoid excesses of evil which hurt yourself or others. Avoid also excesses of good which can turn you into a passive goody-two-shoes that the Witch or Elvira Gulch may abuse. Continuing the examples above:

> Mitch's balanced moral solution was to do his job as best as he could, and not do anything intentionally to hurt his competitors, but concentrate instead on his own performance, i.e. competing with himself. Although his solution is not perfect, he has balanced his "good witches" and his "bad witches" as best as morally possible given the situation.

> Terry's balanced moral solution was to change her tone and manner. Rather than pushing her kids, she chose to expose them to positive role-models they would voluntarily wish to emulate. The kids still feel a little pressure to succeed, but now the "good witches" and the "bad witches" are more balanced.

As Glinda warned Dorothy: *"Never let those ruby slippers off your feet or you'll be at the mercy of the Wicked Witch of the West."* And throughout the story, as the Witch tries to steal back the power of the ruby slippers, it is balance – between her Mind, Heart and Will (Inner Scarecrow, Inner Tin Man and Inner Cowardly Lion) – that Dorothy will draw upon for the journey ahead.

She's no different from all of us.

Without balance, we will never be able to return home to our True Spiritual Selves.

Balanced is how we walk every step of our *Yellow Brick Road*.

## Soul Lesson #9:

## Forgiveness: The Road to Your Inner Wizard.

Dorothy is not going to be safe from the Wicked Witch of the West until she kills her fear of expansion. The entire story, including her journey down *The Yellow Brick Road,* is essentially the story of how she accomplishes that. It's *our* story too, for *The Yellow Brick Road* is a symbol of every human being's spiritual journey towards greater freedom, unlimited expansion, and the discovery – without fear – of our True Power, the Light within us all, *God's Gift* (the meaning of the name *Dorothy*) of being a Soul.

Until now, our Dorothy-Soul has been tutored only by female guides, Glinda and the Wicked Witch of the West. They symbolize two aspects of the *feminine* or *feeling* side of our spiritual journey: *love vs. fear.* On our spiritual path, we either let the love of our Spirit fly, or we resist that love only to experience it as fear. Love or fear, Glinda or the Wicked Witch, is the only emotional choice a human being really makes on their spiritual path; it's an open or shut case.

However, most of the time our emotional battle between love and fear is not an obstacle, but is really just a *reaction*; the conflicted emotions arise secondarily out of our failure to positively *assert* our True Spiritual Selves. Failing to believe in ourselves, failing to demonstrate a high magnitude of faith, we fail to create a sustained, positive momentum. At the first sign of the Wicked Witch, we are pulled down by a kind of spiritual gravity and experience our Inner Light as fear.

Many people who start new enterprises get trapped in this kind of spiritual "push me, pull you"; many new businesses fail because of it; many marriages don't make it past the fifth year because of it. We cripple our opportunity to expand simply by not forcing ourselves to stay focused on expansion, and more expansion – with absolute determination and faith – no matter how many problems come our way. Momentum overcomes fear.

So, to rid ourselves of our fear of Soul Expansion, we must not only master our female or feeling side, but also our *male* or *assertive* side as well. Accessing our male-side, we refuse to allow the Wicked Witch to scare us into defeat or stymie our self-assertion or vigor. Accessing our male-side, we also refuse to overindulge our Glinda-compass by staying overly inward, for even meditation with our Inner Self can be misused as an escape from fear.

Indeed, both aspects of the feminine, fear and love, can be a trap! We must never, ever, forget to positively assert our male-side. We must be positively acting, positively asserting, positively building momentum, positively believing in ourselves, positively enjoying the thrill of the game. That's how we build our Light, stronger and stronger, until it overwhelms, overcomes, and overshadows our fear of expansion completely.

That's why, in the movie, when Dorothy asks Glinda whether she has the power to take her back to Kansas, Glinda responds that it's beyond her power: *"I'm afraid nobody but the Great and Powerful Wizard of Oz will know the way to Kansas."* Only Dorothy's positive male-side, her *Inner Wizard*, has the power to do that.

*"A Wizard? Is he good?,"* asks Dorothy. *"Oh, very good, but very mysterious,"* replies Glinda. *"He lives in the Emerald City, which is very far from here."* Unfortunately, Dorothy does not have a broomstick, itself a phallic symbol of her male power, so she must walk to see the Wizard. This male-side is *"very mysterious"*, because it is foreign to Dorothy who, for most of her life, lived shyly and demurely, until she began to express her Light in a sudden blast of her Toto-Spirit (also a male).

But, unfortunately, Dorothy does not trust this male-side of herself. She still blames herself for hurting Auntie Em, for endangering Toto, for angering the Witch of the West after crushing her sister. We often don't trust this male, willful, spiritous side of ourselves, because we fear it will cause more damage if we let out its Light again. So, we hold back our Light, retreating into our more emotional, feminine side, getting paralyzed between fear and love, rather than asserting our male-side with vitality, strength, self-confidence and spirited focus.

Either we learn to forgive ourselves for any apparent problems we cause others or ourselves when we assert our male-side, or, we cannot, ever, return home to our True Spiritual Selves. We must own our spiritual power, both the female and the male aspects.

We cannot hide from our Light. We must forgive ourselves – radically and completely – for any hurts we believed we caused or any unpleasant experiences that arose in the early stage of expressing our Light. We must forgive ourselves or we will forever be torn between the Good Witch and the Bad Witch, emotionally-shredded into *love vs. fear*, with no place to go but down; then, we will never discover the Power of our Inner Wizard.

*The Yellow Brick Road* is about *forgiveness*: Forgiving yourself for letting out your Light. Forgiving yourself for doubting yourself. Forgiving yourself for hurting others, or rather, provoking their experience of their own hidden hurt.

> Pushing aside fear, and pushing aside love, finally, after 10 years, Kristy bravely asserted her male-side to free herself and her family from her husband's severe alcohol and drug abuse. She refused to hide from it or permit him to hide from it anymore. It eventually led to a divorce. After her children began to suffer from the break-up, Kristy blamed herself. She then shut down her male-side and got trapped be-

tween the emotions of *love vs. fear*. No longer expressing her Light, she became reclusive.

However, two years later, Kristy's husband, suddenly got the wake-up call. He entered an alcoholic counseling program and discovered his own Higher Power, which was part of the program's teaching. After getting his life back in order, he approached Kristy and thanked her for the divorce and the wake-up call. Kristy then forgave herself for her male-side. She realized she had set in motion a cyclone of wicked witches, but that there had been no other way. Kristy forgave herself for unintentionally hurting her kids – who themselves came to their own forgiveness of her – and Kristy began to live again.

When you assert your male-side, in a spirited ejaculation of Soul Power – it can cause problems for others; that's because you are de-stabilizing the status quo and all the wicked witches that have been cackling underneath must face the *Light of Forgiveness*. It takes time before the Light of Forgiveness can disperse the darkness. Like a river that is dammed up with rocks and has gotten muddy, forgiveness removes the rocks; but, it still takes time for the restored flow of the river to wash the mud away. Be patient! Once you begin to access your Inner Wizard, it takes time for Life to re-stabilize at a higher, more powerful, spiritual level.

Pursuing *The Yellow Brick Road* to perfect forgiveness – step by step, in the process of our life – we turn our fear into love, unifying them into a single, powerful, loving, feminine force. Then, we marry this powerful feminine love with an equally powerful male force – until finally, when we touch upon the last brick of the road – we become *whole*. We are no longer conflicted beings composed of good witches or bad, Inner Wizards, Scarecrows, Tin Mans, Lions, Kansans or Totos. We become one single spiritual being, undivided, forgiven of all our inner divisions and "parts", which had only fragmented in the first place when we judged ourselves too harshly.

All the power which had been diverted into these separate divisions now begins to flow in a single, powerful Soul Direction. Through the Power of loving forgiveness, we gain a sense of our spiritual oneness. We begin to mirror the One God, in Whose Image and Likeness – both female and male – we are made. The more we reflect this Oneness, the more the Power of our Inner Wizard will express in our lives.

That's why, symbolically, *The Yellow Brick Road* to forgiveness is yellow. Yellow is the color of *power*, corresponding to the third chakra of the Hindu metaphysical system, the color of our Light Body at the point of our solar plexus, guts, so to speak, like the Buddha's huge belly. Yellow is also the color of gold which represents the male power in the *Kabbalistic* system of Jewish mysticism, the attainment of enlightenment, the *philosopher's gold* in ancient alchemy.

*The Yellow Brick Road* is the path to uncovering, discovering, and recovering your Spiritual Power, by releasing all the misgivings, mis-alignments, and mis-creations of your past.

As in the movie, *The Yellow Brick Road* of forgiveness begins very tightly coiled, a literal knot of yellow bricks – grudges, self-deceptions, blame, guilt, hatred, bitterness, anxiety, regrets, and retribution – of ourselves and others. But then, as you open up to forgiveness, you, like Dorothy, will witness the knot of yellow bricks uncoiling – wider and wider – releasing more and more Power until *The Yellow Brick Road* becomes straight, forceful, assertive, a male-directed line-of-power, fueled by love, pointing directly to the Emerald City.

It is here, you'll fully unveil the Wisdom of Your Inner Wizard. Your male assertive side will fully mature into your inner male-wisdom which, freed from the Witch-of-expansion, combined with Glinda's love, properly balanced by your ruby slippers, will fly you home to your True Self.

Your Inner Wizard awaits you!

To transform our self-hatreds into self-loves. To transform our obstacles into victories. To transform our enemies into allies. To translate the cyclone of events in our life into meaning and understand the lessons they are trying to teach us. To take all our self-judgments and defeats – all our wicked witches – and turn them into self-acceptance and love – this is the unequalled Power of *The Yellow Brick Road* of forgiveness.

Embrace it with feminine love and male fortitude, and, with all your Inner Munchkins cheering you on:

> *"You're off the see the Wizard*
> *The Wonderful Wizard of Oz."*

## Soul Lesson #10:

## Forgiving the Scarecrow: Release the Power of your Mind.

Like Dorothy, once we begin to make our way down *The Yellow Brick Road*, releasing the Power of forgiveness, we will encounter many interesting characters. Indeed, once you've made a commitment to create this kind of forgiveness in your life, if you keep your eyes open, you'll notice that the people you meet symbolize different aspects of your own being – some "fragment" of us that needs to be picked up, regained, forgiven and integrated into us, so we return home to our True Spiritual Self, healed:

> Theodora had been sexually abused by her father at the age of 8; it wrecked her relationships with men. After some spiritual counseling, she decided to forgive this incident, kill her Witch-of-contraction and expand. The next day, "coin-

cidentally", there was a new boss at her job, who, strangely, looked just like her father and acted crudely. On her *Yellow Brick Road*, she was sent a living opportunity to confront the past and heal.

Mitchell had an angry, intolerant mother, who made him afraid to be himself. At the advice of a friend, he went to see a therapist in order to forgive his upbringing, kill the witch, and expand. His mother had "witch-like" dark hair, but his therapist, curiously, had blonde hair. Mitchell had found his Glinda, and his *Yellow Brick Road* was paved.

Each of our encounters with people on *The Yellow Brick Road* are teachers who are sent on our path to help us forgive ourselves. Curiously, even though they are separate individuals, they often appear physically to be "living symbols" of ourselves. That's because forgiveness is truly a Divine path. God coordinates all the people, events, and happenings in your life in a curious "dream", like Dorothy's, to help you forgive and move on.

There are many different teachers for many different matters that need to be forgiven, but, in general, all our teachers on *The Yellow Brick Road* fit into three basic categories: *Mind,* or the Scarecrow. *Heart,* or the Tin Man. *Will,* or the Cowardly Lion.

Dorothy's first teacher on her *Yellow Brick Road* is her Inner Scarecrow, to help her forgive her Mind.

All too often, we blame ourselves for being stupid, for having no brains, for having our *"head all full of stuffin'"* – for making stupid decisions that have wrecked our life. Like nasty, mocking crows, we pick at ourselves, like a worthless bundle of straw, for not having been smart enough to make right decisions in our life: "Why did I do this?" "How could I think the way I did?" "Why did I make so many mistakes?" "If only I had done this instead." "If only I had gotten an education." Or, we may also pick at the brains of others, "What an idiot!" "How did I hook up with them?" "He can't think his way out of a paper bag."

Whether you judge yourself for being stupid, or judge someone else, makes no difference. On *The Yellow Brick Road*, everyone is each other's mirror of forgiveness; any judgement towards another person exposes your own judgement within yourself:

> Wendy took a job as a teller in a local bank. Her boss was a kind woman, but seemed very slow, and muddled. Yet, she was constantly criticizing Wendy for how slowly she did her job. Wendy was furious, because the woman was "so dumb".

> Having been on *The Yellow Brick Road* of forgiveness for a while, Wendy realized she was really angry at her ex-husband who was, she thought, incredibly dim-witted at making a living. She was also angry at herself for being "so dumb" to have married him.

She forgave her ex-husband, and herself, and her strained relationship with her boss suddenly morphed into a friendship, with *Oz magic*.

That's the Power of forgiveness! Past judgements, past decisions, stupid, ridiculous choices – all the straw-picking crows in our Mind – have to be forgiven or our Inner Scarecrow will stays stuck in a cornfield and will never discover its brilliance!

Our Mind is a powerful tool. We can use it as the Scarecrow sang, to *"wile away the hours, consulting with the flowers, talking to the rain."* Our Mind gives human beings enormous control over the natural elements; with our Mind, we build houses, cars; we transport oranges in the dead of winter.

Our human Mind, reflecting the Intelligence in Whose Image and Likeness we are made, gives us Power to shape our earthly existence. It gives us, what the Bible calls *dominion* or *stewardship* over the earth – to *subdue it* and utilize nature for human needs. It allows us to peer into the actual mechanics of the universe and discover the relationship between matter and energy, $E=MC^2$ – as Einstein formulated it. We can actually understand "how God did it"!

Our Mind also gives us dominion over *our* nature – the personal direction, choices, and experiences of each of our earthly, human lives.

Our Mind allows us to vault the heavens on high, with noble ideas and values: *"With the thoughts you'd be think'in, you could be another Lincoln,"* sang Dorothy to the freed-up Scarecrow.

All of the deep, spiritual Truths of the Soul, which are embedded and veiled behind the superficial material reality of Life, can be released through the piercing acumen of an insightful Mind. This is how the greatest religious scriptures, the Bible, the Qur'an, the Rig Veda and others, came about, through Enlightened, Light-Illuminated, Revelatory Minds such as Christ, Moses, Muhammad, Buddha, Krishna and others.

Moreover, our Mind has the extraordinary power of imagination, of concrete visualization. It allows us to *focus* the Creative Power of our Inner Munchkin, rendering it even more powerful. Not only can we playfully dream of unfathomable Oz possibilities like a child, but we can also – harnessing the Power of our adult mind – *choose* out of all the possibilities, the possibilities that excite us.

Focusing our mental power on these possibilities, energizing them, we turn our dreams into reality. Just think what the power of the human Mind has created: rockets to the moon, toasters, shoes, glass for windows, ice cream… It is human nature to take our imagination – our ability to image or picture – and turn our Munchkin fantasies into reality. You can accomplish the seemingly impossible with the Illumined Power of a correctly functioning Mind.

However, there are some "kinks" in the functioning of our Mind which prevent us from utilizing its Divine gifts. These kinks appear almost immediately after Dorothy happens upon our Scarecrow in the movie. Dorothy reaches a crossroad, where she has an alternative: two completely different, seemingly contrary paths on *The Yellow Brick Road* reveal themselves; both go to the Emerald City, but Dorothy does not know which to take.

The Scarecrow, quick to help Dorothy out, responds, *"That way is a very nice way." "It's pleasant down that way too." "Of course, people do go both ways."* But Dorothy is flustered, because the Scarecrow, symbolizing the limitations of her own rational Mind, cannot help her.

Why do our rational minds experience such conflicts?

First, Life cannot be fathomed by the rational mind alone! At any moment of time – if you fully embrace your Oz freedom and have not saddled yourself into too many Kansan rationalizations – there are literally billions of possibilities, billions of choices you can make. You are, as a Soul, quite free to do virtually *anything* you want (provided it is good and loving). That's how much Freedom, God's Own Unlimited, Unrestricted Nature, resides in you.

So, it's not easy to make up our Mind and decide which Soul Route to take. One road to the Emerald City will bring you one set of adventures; another road, will bring you a completely different set. I myself, a particularly dumb Scarecrow, started out thinking I wanted to be a lawyer, then went to medical school, then entered advertising, then entered the clergy, and then began writing books like this, all in the process of one Soul trying to unravel its destiny.

Confusing paths confound our Mind because our minds are very much like personal computers; our Mind can only do computations based on its programming. For our brain, the most advanced "personal computer" ever made, such programming consists of *beliefs*. We may believe one thing, with one portion of our Scarecrow Mind, and another thing with another portion of our Scarecrow Mind. We may have completely contradictory beliefs which cause us, like Dorothy, to face seemingly contradictory paths to the Emerald City.

If you do an honest Soul Search of your Inner Scarecrow's programming, you will notice many crossroads resulting from many confused and contrary belief systems. Unknot them in your Mind before you live them out in the flesh, and it can save you a lot of pain and suffering.

Like all the characters Dorothy will meet on *The Yellow Brick Road,* there's really nothing wrong with our Inner Scarecrow except that he lacks *confidence* – from the Latin *confidere, with faith*. Indeed, even a seemingly nitwitted Scarecrow was able to figure out how to outsmart some disgruntled apple trees, provoking them to throw their apples at Dorothy and himself, so they could collect them.

The more you use your Mind, the more you will be able to successfully face the challenges of *The Yellow Brick Road*. You will be able to treat these challenges as a kind of gymnasium to train the two lobes of your cerebral "muscle". This will help you develop the more unified *Oz State of Mind*, so you can experience even more confidence — faith — in the Divine gift of your Mind. Soon, you won't consider yourself a dumb Scarecrow anymore.

The more faith you have in your Mind, the more the Power of your Inner Scarecrow will reveal itself. Like the Scarecrow in the movie, your Mind will become the protector of your Dorothy-Soul as you journey to meet your Inner Wizard.

1. A Forgiving Mind, freed from all self-doubt

2. A Unified Mind, freed from conflicting beliefs

3. A One-Pointed Mind, focused in a single clear Soul Direction

These are three ways to release the brilliance of your Inner Scarecrow. These are the three main Mind-gates into the Emerald City.

Like Dorothy in the movie, always walk down *The Yellow Brick Road* with your Scarecrow, arm in arm…

"To Oz?"

"To Oz!"

## Soul Lesson # 11:

### Forgiving the Tin Man: The Gift of a Loving Heart

All the scattered minds of our Inner Scarecrow can never harmonize unless the voice of our True Heart gets heard.

Indeed, our Heart can go a whole lifetime not getting heard – as if, like the Tin Man, our lips have rusted shut. Drenched by reigning opinions, false pieties, and distorted beliefs passed off as Truth, our True Heart can disappear from our chest. Instead of a clear, rhythmic, heartbeat we hear an empty rumble… rumble… rumble.

Once you start down *The Yellow Brick Road*, it isn't long before you must learn to forgive that cold, galvanized, mechanized version of yourself, that "artificial person" that, in some measure, you had become in order to survive in the Kansan world. This is the side you manufactured in order to interact with all the Kansans and maintain a "safe distance" inside your tin-cocoon, so you could "just be you".

But now, this tin-cocoon must be released and forgiven. Dorothy might not have torn away from Kansas so forcefully and hurtfully, had she let out her Heart's desire sooner. Many of our mistakes might never have taken place, had we not imprisoned the Voice of our True Heart:

*"Oil can… Oil can,"* strains the lip-rusted Tin Man. At first Dorothy and the Scarecrow do not even understand what he is saying. But, after deciphering the mumble, they promptly surmise what the galvanized guy is saying and apply the unction to loosen his lips. *"Ahh"* … sighs the Tin Man, begging them to oil and free every one of his limbs and joints.

This is what happens to every one of us when we don't pay attention to our Heart. This is what happens to all of us when our mouths rust and we fail to express our Heart's desires openly. We contract. We freeze. We tighten up. Just look at Life in our galvanized, metal-plated material world. Look at the number of people suffering from clenched backaches, gripping headaches, and knee-cementing arthritis! They've become immobile physically, because their Hearts have been immobile emotionally.

Unlike so many of our body parts which come in dualistic pairs, our Heart is centrally located and singular, symbolizing its spiritual importance. When we don't act from our Heart and don't live Life according to its impulses, then our entire life, like the Tin Man's body, starts to creak. We lose spontaneity. We prematurely age at any age. If you've ever been with someone who has not aged gracefully, you will generally notice that, for whatever reason, they have not lived from their Heart.

But, if you are with an "elderly person" who has lived from the Heart, you will notice something miraculous: Their eyes sparkle. There's a lilt to their voice. You can rarely hear a complaint pass their lips. They are fascinated with new ideas, new ways of thinking. They are open and generous. They continue to grow and evolve. Youth abounds in them, no matter what their physical age or state.

As the Tin Man sang: *"I could stay young and chipper, and I'd lock it with a zipper, if I only had a heart."*

Your Heart is the central beacon for the Life Force which powers all Life. Indeed, this is the most powerful force in the entire universe: *Love.* As you grow spiritually, and you increasingly experience the Grace that comes from the *Oz State of Mind*, you cannot help but come to an astonishing observation. Everything we experience on *The Yellow Brick Road* of Life is a form of Love. Think about it.

### Anger is a form of Love

Anger is how Love feels when the Love, for whatever reason, has violated your personal space and your Self-love puts up a boundary.

### Envy is a form of Love

Envy is how Love feels when you love something someone else has, but you withhold love from yourself by not believing you can have it.

**Jealousy is a form of a Love**

Jealousy is how Love feels when you love something someone else has and wish them harm, because they have it and you don't.

**Fear is a form of a Love**

As we've already seen, fear is how Love feels when you resist or are blocked from expressing the Light of your true desires. Fear also protects your body from danger and is therefore God's Love.

**Hate is a form of Love**

Hate is how Love feels when you desire something so much, you can't stand its power over you, and so you want it wiped out.

The list is endless. If you look at every single one of your feelings, even the so-called "unloving" ones, you will find that they are all Love disguised.

We travel down *The Yellow Brick Road*, arm-in-arm with our Inner Tin Man, simply to express Love as Love and to forgive, release, and transform any of its degraded expressions into a Purer Love that more closely resembles that Love which is the very Nature of God. We travel down *The Yellow Brick Road* to develop that cardinal virtue which is the height of the Divine Expression of Love: *Compassion*.

The word *compassion* comes from the Latin meaning *with passion*; *passion* comes from the Latin root word *patir* meaning *to suffer*. Compassion means the capacity to feel another person's suffering as if it were your own. It is the ability to empathize deeply with someone else's troubles and pains. When your Inner Tin Man is compassionate, you have the ability to deeply comprehend another's emotional make up. You become exquisitely sensitive to the very humanness of another person. Recognizing this humanness as your very own, softens the all-too-human tendency to judge others "right" or "wrong", which is the #1 cause of a scattered Inner Scarecrow.

Compassion reaches out from the human heart and embraces not merely other human beings, but all Life on the planet, including natural enemies: *"I'd be friends with the sparrow and the boy who shoots the arrows, if I only had a heart,"* croons the Tin Man. A truly compassionate heart can sense, compassionately, the Divine Love which makes up all living beings and all Life on our earth.

For our Inner Tin Man, there is no easy route to develop heartfelt compassion. Polluted by so many distorted and manipulative Kansan emotions, it is a very difficult task – far more difficult than bringing back a simple broomstick. Every Dorothy-Soul must be absolutely devoted to the task of turning each beat of his/her heart in the correct direction, so that it loves with increasing lovingness. How? A few basic suggestions, straight from the heart:

**Do unto others that which you would have them do unto you.**

This is such common advice, it now sounds like religious cliché. The converse is also true: That which is hateful to you, do not do to another. This *Golden Rule* can be found in virtually every single major world religion. It works.

**Be the first to love.**

In any situation where love is being expressed unlovingly, take spiritual responsibility to change the interaction and set it on a loving course. This is a powerful technique that will set your compassionate heart free.

**Lastly, but actually firstly – Love yourself.**

Those Tin Men or Tin Women who have difficulty loving other people usually have difficulty loving themselves and project that on others. True Self-love is never selfish, because it recognizes others on *The Yellow Brick Road* – even the Witch — as a mirror of Self-love, however distorted.

Every Tin Man has a Heart, no matter how hollow our chest may sound at times. But few of us have ever taken the time or done the spiritual work to fully develop our Heart Power.

Our physical heart pulses, beat by beat, moment by moment, sending blood filled with oxygen, food, and everything we possibly need to sustain life, to every cell of our body. But, beyond the physical heart, is our

Spiritual Heart. Mystics testify that it exists on a more subtle, invisible level of reality which is only visible to the clairvoyant amongst us. So, in this sense, you could say that our True Heart, like the Tin Man's, is missing from us all. To make our Spiritual Heart visible – so it becomes real to us and others – is what all of us Tin Folk must do on our *Yellow Brick Road.*

Our life will continue to appear merely material, a man-made, clanking, hunk of junk, with no purpose and meaning – until we exercise the spiritual muscle we were born with, and pump Love through our life.

*"Lub dub… Lub dub… Lub dub"* Can you hear your own heart beating?

If not, listen more closely.

## Soul Lesson # 12:

## Forgiving your Cowardly Lion: Finding True Courage

The last of Dorothy's three companions is the hardest of all to forgive. The Cowardly Lion, who represents our Will, appears to be a full-maned, ferocious beast, roaring at our Inner Scarecrow, causing our tin knees to knock, rampaging after our "defenseless" little Toto-Spirit. But the moment he does, Dorothy walks right over to him and raps him on his paws, as a momma cat might do to a baby kitten: *"Shame on you…,"* Dorothy scolds. Then, his ferocious roar dissolves into tiny tears, as the Cowardly Lion begins to wipe his eyes with his tail.

Our Inner Cowardly Lion may make a display of ferocity and grandstanding Will, but this display is superficial. Underneath, we have not forgiven the low self-esteem and the lack of belief in ourselves which fuels its falsity. This inner psychic weakness is what really makes us fearful of control by others. All the people to whom we are beholding, all the people from whom we can't escape because their love is so smothering or conditional – their power really comes from the fact that we have failed to forgive and free the lion-sized Will of our Inner Cowardly Lion.

Our Inner Cowardly Lion cannot heal our emotional pussy-footing, because there is a part of us that actually *likes* being cowardly. Our pathetic cowardice hooks all sorts of maternal responses from the people around us and draws all sorts of pity, love, tenderness, and caresses from others. Our Inner Cowardly Lion actually becomes addicted to all the energy we pry out of other people; we become hooked on our feigned cowardly behavior. Being a "scaredy-cat" becomes a theatrical act. Our inner selves watch ourselves manipulate, while we skillfully assert our Will – not directly, but instead, through passive-aggressive behavior – to get our emotional pay off. This is how we turn our powerful Lion inside-out:

> Trevor had an older brother in the film industry where he also worked as a screenwriter.
>
> He had, for most of his life, lived under his brother's shadow. Although Trevor was enormously talented, his Cowardly Lion prevented him from equaling or surpassing his brother's success. Every time he got close to major success, he sabotaged himself. Inwardly, he was afraid that if he permitted himself to let out his roar, his older brother wouldn't love him; he had spent his entire life wanting his older

> brother's love and approval. His Cowardly Lion was designed to keep him "weak", "young" and "less powerful", with the hopes that his brother would always "take him under his wing" and give him the love and care he craved.

To forgive the inverted use of our Will, to forgive our very manipulative Cowardly Lion, requires us to dig very deep into the most primitive, animal-like aspects of our nature.

Because the human being is an animal (and the Cowardly Lion is Dorothy's only Oz-animal companion) we often have a cowardice that's actually built into our physical nature for the purpose of survival. We may be afraid of being over-powered, attacked, even being eaten alive, deep vital fears we share with many in the animal kingdom. Even though we are not living in a real jungle like the Cowardly Lion, we may react to the normal experiences of our "civilized jungle" as if we were:

> We may react to the loss of money as if it is a real physical threat to our survival, including actual starvation – even though it is a momentary dip in the stock market.

> We may react to our spouse's "bad mood" with hostility, because our sex drive seems automatically programmed to react to any lack-of-receptivity in our partner with aggression – even though it's really just an awful day at the office.

> We may react to a new employee with competitive aggression, even animal-posturing, as if they are going to plunder the scarce food resources in the forest and hurt our nest — even though he/she's been hired to make our job easier.

"Honey, it's a jungle out there!" That's how our Inner Cowardly Lion often reacts to situations, with basic, raw, animal instinct.

But underneath all these deep vital fears stands one major fear – a whopper – which must be completely forgiven, or we cannot progress further on *The Yellow Brick Road*, our wills forever paralyzed by cowardice. This fear is *the* fear of all fears – hooded, with scimitar in hand: *Death!*

Every major fear we Souls have is fear of death in disguise. Fear of poverty is the fear of "death" of our bodies. Fear of not having a relationship is fear of loss of life i.e. death. Fear of not having children is a fear of death of the entire species. Fear of expansion is, at its core, a fear of death, as the Witch makes threateningly clear in her menacing way.

There is not one single major religion or spiritual discipline that does not make the releasing of our human Soul from fear of death paramount. Whether it is the resurrection of the dead in Christianity, Judaism. or certain Greek Mystery cults – whether it is reincarnation in Hinduism, Mysticism or New Age spirituality – whether it is *Nirvana* in the Buddhist tradition or Paradise in Islam – the loosening of our animal fear of death is a spiritual necessity to free the Power of our Lion's Will from all its mortal fears and cowardice.

Focusing your Will on facing death – becoming *"a li–yon not a mow-ess,"* as the Cowardly Lion sang – is essential if you are going to permanently anchor the *Oz State of Mind*. Focusing your Will on unknotting your fears and phobias around death is the most freeing thing you can do for your Soul.

Virtually every limitation you experience in life, virtually every obstacle you create on the journey down your *Yellow Brick Road*, is, in some fashion, a veiled fear of death built into your Inner Scarecrow's programming. Once you de-program the fear of death, all these limitations and phobias often collapse like a house of cards. You are set footloose and fancy free down your *Yellow Brick Road*. All the energy of your Lion's rage, all the willfulness that's been hidden under your fake displays of cowardice will be released outwardly. Your previous raw animal fear will be channeled into developing one of the most critical of all spiritual goals: *True Courage*.

All Cowardly Lions, who discover their True Courage, cease to trust any authority, whether witch, wizard, mortal or other, as the overlord of their Soul. They only absolutely trust God and God's Power in themselves. True Courage sees all people, and all institutions, as simply different "human forms" of power – not as the Ultimate Power Behind the Universe. Lions with True Courage, while respecting others – including family or authorities – do not consider them to be God and so never permit their Will to be overpowered or detoured from what their Soul needs to accomplish.

A Lion with True Courage, while always cooperating to further human endeavors, is always true to him/herself, and is always operating at a higher moral and spiritual level, like Joan of Arc or Nelson Mandela. This is courage that knows the Truth, seeks the Truth, declares the Truth, even in the face of death: *True Courage*.

At first, True Courage seems like bravery or even *bravado*, because we seem to be going against the crowd, sometimes fearfully. But True Courage is not really brave at all. It is really a quiet, spiritual *knowingness* – a simple, self-assured sense of "what must be done," "what must be walked through," and "what our Will must accomplish" for the sake of Truth. True Courage is quietly earth-shaking!

True Courage is true selfless devotion to serving others with lessened emphasis on oneself. When you demonstrate True Courage, it indicates that you've been spiritually transformed. You are no longer a mere creature of nature, running from pain, drawn towards pleasure — but a *spiritual animal*, made in God's Image and Likeness. You have truly become *human* – an animal that is capable of expressing God's Will through your Will – a "king" (or "queen") of the Forest.

We all have a Cowardly Lion inside us. We indulge our fears. We lick our paws. We weep and moan about how awful, sleepless and worthless we are. But, every Dorothy must forgive his antics. They are just the whimpers of an insecure Kansan kitty. Once, we were all scared and dependent, mere lion cubs. However, it's time to grow up and put that aside. It's time to *roar!* To roar at the top of our lungs!

Release the flames of Leo. Feel the lion-sized pride of a strong, solid, focused Will. Let others hear the mighty roar of the King of the Forest in you. Know that the Lion in you knows no fear of death and is therefore totally free to live.

Nothing will hold you back from the Emerald City – not even the Witch's spell – once you forgive your cowardice and find your True Courage.

## Soul Lesson #13:

## Beware of Poisoned Poppies: The Danger of False Ego

To shed your cowardice and let out your Lion's roar is good, positive, and proud, provided you are doing so in a way that is spiritually-aligned to the purpose of your Soul and is not destructive to either yourself or another person. However, the shadow side of the Lion in you, is one of the most dangerous pitfalls on your *Yellow Brick Road:* Excessive, destructive, false *ego*.

Ego itself is not a bad thing. We all have an ego, a sense of "I-ness", a sense that we are conscious, that we are an "entity", an *individual*. The ego, in its true state, is really just a personal awareness of the uniqueness of our Soul in relationship to the uniqueness of others, our "sense of self". When someone violates your spiritual nature, a healthy ego will jump to defend you; when you do something that empowers your spiritual advancement, a healthy ego will know it and reward you with self-praise. A healthy ego is a very powerful, good helper.

Without an ego, Dorothy would have stayed in Kansas and never ventured forth *Somewhere Over the Rainbow*. Indeed, while she was in Kansas, under the laborious thumb of Auntie Em, stuck on the boring gray farm, she did not demonstrate a healthy ego at all. Her ego was actually beaten down and squelched by the group. That's a sick ego.

Today, there are many spiritual movements that demand that you "give up your ego", but this is a very dangerous thing. People who vacate their ego often end up participating in religious cults. They don't really lose ego; they simply substitute the ego of the cult or cult-leader for their own. This is equally true of people who substitute the ego of a CEO or corporation for their own, or those who substitute the ego of a political leader, maybe a Hitler, for their own. This also happens in marriages, where one partner permits the other's ego to dominate. They lose their spiritual center. They have their compass of Goodness diverted. Their Inner Glinda becomes sidetracked, because other egos have overshadowed their own.

Your ego is a prized possession. As long as it is properly aligned to the purpose and the intention of your True Self, it is an ally. However, beware of the ego when it is not properly aligned to your True Self. Then, all hell can break out.

On the final stretch to the Emerald City, it seems as if everything is perfect:

Dorothy, representing our Soul, is focused on her goal, with no apparent fear of the Witch-of-expansion.

Toto, representing Dorothy's Spirit, is yapping along, positively encouraging her. There's no threat to self-expression or creativity.

Our Inner Scarecrow isn't scattered; our Tin Man is loose and chipper; our Cowardly Lion is prideful and perky. You'd never know they had any doubts left.

Everyone's happily skipping down *The Yellow Brick Road.*

But, then – right then – the Wicked Witch of the West, spying on them through her crystal ball, chooses that moment to pounce: "*Poppies… poppies will make them sleep,*" she croaks.

Upon a field covered with beautiful red poppies, the flower-source of opium, the Witch sprinkles her poison. Soon, Dorothy, Toto and the Cowardly Lion fall asleep. Near dead in a stupor, in a state of utter unconsciousness, the journey to the Emerald City seems over. Dorothy's hope of knowing her Inner Wizard, the male knowledge she needs to supplement her Inner Glinda and return home to her True Self, has been put to sleep.

The sickening "envy green" of the Dorothy's Inner Witch has not yet been purified into pure, sparkling, *emerald* green! It will be, soon.

It is a common spiritual experience. The moment your Soul feels most powerful, most pulled-together, most integrated between your Mind, Heart, Will, and Spirit – then, something happens to put you right back in your place. The more you make spiritual progress, the more you can feel as if you are on top of the world. You can get an exhilarating sense of spiritual power, of your Soul Connection to God, feeling and seeing the fluid, Grace-full "coincidence coordination" of the *Oz State of Mind*. But then, without realizing it, catching you unaware – indeed, intoxicated – your ego can get a little cocky:

> Brian was a brilliant financier who was climbing the corporate ladder at a major banking chain.
>
> As a child he had been seriously put down by "the guys" for being a "wimp". But when he entered his chosen career, he swore that no one was going to put him down again.
>
> He pushed aside all his fears, single-mindedly focused his Mind, Heart, Will and Spirit, towards success – and soon, he discovered his Power: He shot up the ladder at record speed. However, while doing so, his ego was also getting bigger and bigger, falser and falser – until one day, "for no reason", in spite of his amazing successes, he was overlooked for the presidency and they hired someone from the outside. Brian crashed! The put-down child in him surfaced and he fell into a serious depression.

Underneath bloated, false, egos is usually a lot of "hot air" which has been super-heated by anger. As you spiritually advance down your *Yellow Brick Road*, and you realize that you have creative control over your life and can choose the experiences you want to create – oftentimes, you don't realize all the rage and anger that's still inside you, left over from when Kansans were still in control of your Soul. One little taste of spiritual power, and you think you are the Master of Life, only to find yourself knocked unconscious by the poppy poison of the Witch-of-expansion.

Fueling all false, destructive, controlling egos is enormous, fiery, hate-filled anger, the shadow side of the Cowardly Lion, if not of the entire astrological sign of Leo. On your *Yellow Brick Road*, this rage must be forgiven completely.

"Help... Help... ," cried the Scarecrow and the Tin Man helplessly, realizing that their companions' somnolence was a spell from the Wicked Witch; fortunately, because they were not fleshly, they were unaffected by the poppies.

Then, Glinda appears, compassionately superimposed over the scene. With a majestic wave of her magic wand, it begins to snow: Pure, white, freezing snow – just the thing to cool the anger and "hot air" of a bloated ego – begins to fall on the poppy field. Our *Yellow Brick Road* travelers awaken, thanks to the compass correction of the Witch of the North.

On your *Yellow Brick Road*, stay alert. There are a number of signs that your ego has gotten false; here are just a few:

1. You often power trip on others, even in the guise of "helping them".

2. You begin to think you are always right.
3. You are always giving people advice, even when they don't ask for it.
4. You believe you are already enlightened and forget that the only Perfect Being is God.
5. Your value system becomes distorted; you become overly concerned about what others think about you and gauge yourself by their opinions — or ignore their opinions entirely.

At the first sign of any of the above, wave Glinda's magic wand and apply a healthy blizzard to your Soul:

1. Compassionately, remember when you were confused and lost and needed help. Remind yourself that other people are Souls, just like you.
2. Remind yourself that although the Presence of God is in you, you are not God in Totality. Your Power comes from a relationship with God; it's not yours alone.
3. Always make sure your heart is well-focused on selfless service and love. Periodically do "self-checks" to make sure you are not unconsciously manipulating others.
4. Open your ears and listen more! You will find you've got a lot to learn from Souls who are supposedly less advanced on *The Yellow Brick Road*.

5. Laugh at yourself. There is a tendency, because of religious programming, to be deathly serious about spiritual matters. Imagine God with a sense of humor. Enjoy making mistakes and stop trying to be so perfect; that's usually a cover-up for anger.

Some of the most spiritually illumined and gifted people in the world have fallen into the ego-trap; not a few of them, at the height of their fame, have ended up deported or in jail. It's a human problem. Why? Because, we've got such enormous spiritual power in us, being *Made in the Image and Likeness of God*, that we can easily get side-tracked by false ego.

On your *Yellow Brick Road*, the more you unveil the hidden powers of your Mind, Heart, Will and Spirit, the more you must guard against false ego and falling asleep. You must stay on guard until you have permanently anchored the *Oz State of Mind*.

*The Yellow Brick Road* is a conscious path to Spiritual Power, requiring you to always be clear, self-reflective, and honest about your ego's relationship with others and yourself. Becoming unconscious of the state of your ego – the poison of poppies – is therefore serious; it threatens the success of the entire earthly journey of your Soul.

Who is the Witch-of-expansion? Now, you know her completely. Now you know her power. She is your false ego! Never, ever, fall under her spell!

## Soul Lesson #14:

## The Emerald City: Purification and Surrender

Once you've forgiven your Mind, Heart, and Will, befriending your Inner Scarecrow, Inner Tin Man, Inner Cowardly Lion, you've accomplished the basics of conscious forgiveness. There's always more forgiveness that can take place; in fact, it's a never-ending process. However now, like Dorothy in the story, you've reached a new plateau in your spiritual development. You've reached the Emerald City. There it is, right ahead, gleaming in green.

Green is the color of the fourth chakra in the Hindu metaphysical system. It's the color of Divine Heart, the color of our Light Body as it appears at the location of our physical heart; hence green is also the color of Divine Love or a Compassionate Life, all the beautiful and glorious vegetation on the planet.

To be bathed in green is to become spiritually refreshed and renewed, as you feel when lying on fresh green grass: green means the restoration of your Natural Spiritual Self, your Soul-on-earth.

Our Inner Dorothy, our Soul, is about to receive the green power of emeralds: improved relationships, relaxation, deepened connection to one's Soul, purification, and strengthened spiritual insight. However, to receive this gift of Spirit, our Soul must participate in an *intentional community*, real people like us who are similarly devoted to the spiritual path of anchoring the *Oz State of Mind*:

*"Ding… Dong,"* sounds the bell, as our comrades tug on the cord. Immediately, a curious fellow peeks his head out of the little window high upon the door. Immediately, he starts bawling them out for not paying attention to the sign: *"Bell Out of Order. Please knock."* – which, for some reason, had not been posted. After he petulantly posts it, he retreats through the window. Then, Dorothy proceeds to knock as requested and our odd fellow ridiculously reappears.

Announcing with great brazenness, *"We've come to the see the Wizard,"* the odd fellow is stunned. *"But nobody can see the great Oz. Nobody's **ever** seen the great Oz. Even I've never seen him."* However, after seeing that it was the Witch of the North who had sent Dorothy – as evidenced by the ruby slippers – the fellow changes his mind, and they immediately gain entrance to the Emerald City.

As Dorothy and her comrades enter the Emerald City, we notice that the people there are more refined and sophisticated. They are not as tiny or quirky as Munchkins. They are full-sized, respectable adults, representing the fact that our Souls, after following *The Yellow Brick Road* of forgiveness, have spiritually matured. Forgiveness matures us, because we let go of the past, our Kansan childhood. Through forgiveness, you grow up!

Almost all maturing Souls must forge some kind of spiritual connection with an intentional spiritual community. It can be a church, mosque, ashram, synagogue or some well-minded secular society. But, it can also be a group of like-minded people, friends, who share your path, so you can empower each other. Although our spiritual journey often starts off as an individual, no one has just an individual path. Any spiritual journey, while including us individually, also transcends us – and indeed includes the entire world, all people and all Life in it. No one can go it alone.

An intentional community serves to "re-parent" us, "re-school" us, "re-socialize" us, and more correctly "re-program" us according to the more spiritual ways of Oz. In a sense, we take on a new family. Our Soul undergoes a kind of *rebirth*, a *purification* – one of the powers of emeralds. Indeed, this is exactly what happens to Dorothy and her companions. They undergo a deep spiritual cleansing, not unlike baptism, circumcision, the laying on of hands, and many analogous rituals:

> "Rub, rub here. Rub, rub there. Whether you're tin or bronze. That certain air of savoir faire, in the merry old land of Oz." "Can you even dye my eyes to

*match my gown?,"* queries Dorothy. *"Jolly Ole' Town,"* she sings, after her Emerald City cosmetician nods affirmatively.

Such a purification, with the help of an intentional community, can further raise the Powers of your Mind, Heart, Will and Spirit, bringing your Soul to a new level of Oz awareness. It's not uncommon for Souls at this point to take on a new identity, maybe even a new name, as in Hinduism, Islam, Christianity, and many different religions. The dull, gray remnants of Kansas are cleansed. Residual guilt and self-recrimination, the dirt and grime from the exhausting journey of forgiveness down *The Yellow Brick Road* is washed away. The new spiritual peer group of our Emerald City bestows its recognition upon us and we begin to see our new spiritual selves through the fresher, clearer eyes of others. We feel good. We feel free.

With this however, there is danger – more false ego. The power of an intentional community (especially a highly-evolved one that's supportive of us and becomes "our new parents") can sometimes dwarf our individual sense of ourselves, reducing us back to being more advanced, but still psychologically dependent, children. We can begin to think that the fabulous citizens of the Emerald City are the "end all" to spiritual development and we can dissolve our ego into theirs. Our authentic spiritual need for community can dissolve into spiritually dangerous cultism.

There is also a false ego danger that we can become intensely "addicted" to the ease, comfort, pampering and support we get from our spiritual peer group, and not continue evolving on our path. Others may also become obsessively-compulsively reliant upon the purification rituals of their intentional community, seeking repeated baptisms, repeated sin cleansings over and over and over again. This is a spiritual sign that there is a severe guilt problem and it needs professional psychotherapeutic attention.

So, just when Dorothy, Toto and her three companions have been anointed, cleansed, purged, and are in delightful communion with their Emerald City hosts, their false egos are unexpectedly challenged again, to help them grow further:

"SURRENDER DOROTHY," we see the Wicked Witch of the West scrawling in the sky, skywriting with her broomstick. But, surrender here does not mean give up and permit our fears – our Witch-within – to win, waving a white flag of defeat. The *surrender* the Witch is challenging Dorothy to learn about, is one of the most profound spiritual teachings.

*Surrender* comes from the Old French *to give up*. But you're not giving up as in defeat – you're giving UP! UP! You're letting go and letting God, as the popular expression goes. You are relinquishing control and seeking skyward, permitting a Higher Power to descend and free you from your remaining, threatening, false ego.

When you surrender, you put your Mind, Heart, Will and Spirit secondary to God. You open all your faculties to the Grace or Providence you need to guide you through any challenge in Life. You surrender completely to your God Self, so that God can take over your mortal self. You permit yourself peace and relaxation – another emerald power – even in the face of a threat, trusting that God will help you. Thus, true spiritual surrender is not defeat, but guaranteed victory!

Robin and Butch had marriage problems, which they were not able to solve. At the height of the problem, *The Yellow Brick Road* sent them a threat from the Witch-of-expansion: Robin was offered the "job of her lifetime" in Chicago. Butch was, "coincidentally", offered "a major career move" in Boston. To be themselves, they had to split up, symbolic of the power struggle in the marriage for over 15 years.

After coming to spiritual counseling, they were advised, after long discussion (because both seriously wanted their marriage to be saved) to SURRENDER. Both were asked to simultaneously give UP these new positions, despite the money and status. *Letting go and letting God,* they permitted God to lead them down *The Yellow Brick Road* of forgiveness and reconciliation.

It took time, and a lot of separate learning for each of them down *The Yellow Brick Road,* but soon – amazingly to both of them – in about a month, both were sent major opportunities. In fact, these opportunities were actually better than they had before, and cozily within a 35 mile radius from their current home.

Surrendering their Wicked Witch – the fear that one would control or diminish the other's success, a common marital problem in today's era,

God was able to take over. They stopped resisting the Witch. Surrendering to her, they converted their fears to Love. A creative solution to their two-career marriage came because they were open – fully surrendered – to the *Oz State of Mind*, their connection to God. They stopped putting their individual fears and egos before their shared Love. So, they healed individually and together as a couple.

No matter how far we've come on the journey, we must all surrender to our last remaining witch-fear and false ego, in order to face them and rise above them. By surrendering completely to our fears, we cease to resist them at all, so they can be converted to the pure green, spiritually refreshing, light of emeralds, Divine Love and Compassion. Then we are restored to our Natural (Green) Spiritual Selves. Thus, surrendering could be said to be the final stage of purification.

Purification means the restoration to the pure state of your Soul. But, as the denizens of the Emerald City teach us, this is *always* in relationship to *others*. Therefore, purification always goes hand-in-hand with surrender and vice-versa.

*The Yellow Brick Road* must never be just about your personal journey alone. It must never become a self–indulgent, navel-meditating, closed-in, exclusively-personal forgiveness "trip". It must always be open to the Light and Love of your mates, your friends, your relatives, your acquaintances, your neighborhood, your nation, your world.

Indeed, it must be open to *all humankind, and all Life on our planet,* if not beyond. This is the "intentional community" to which we *all* belong. This is the "intentional community" we must all serve.

The Emerald City is our world! We've got to save it, to save ourselves.

## Soul Lesson #15:

## Meeting the Wizard: Bringing Back the Broomstick

After the Witch's threat, Dorothy and her cohorts approach the guard who is protecting the entrance to the *inner chamber* of the Wizard. Petitioning him to see the great Oz, they quickly receive a rude response: *"The Wizard says go away!"*

Then Dorothy, believing her entire journey has failed, collapses in tears: *"I thought I was on my way home. Auntie Em was so good to me. And I never appreciated it, running away and hurting her feelings. Professor Marvel said she was sick. She may be dying. And it's all my fault. I'll never forgive myself. Never… Never."*

On the threshold of meeting the Wizard, *The Fake Professor of guilt* shows itself again, even more forcefully and even more fake. Indeed, the deeper we go towards complete surrender (the *inner chamber*) of our fears and guilt, the worse these can seem and the more forcefully these Inner Witches can materialize in the events and circumstances in our lives. Our guilt can go from being a mild-mannered Professor Marvel, to a flame-fuming, nose-smoking, Wizard. That's because, on your *Yellow Brick Road,* that's exactly what your Soul must confront. How can you confront your deepest guilt and fear, and turn them to Love, unless you face them squarely through Life?

> Ned was miserable and wanted to give up the secure job he had at the automobile factory. But, with the sole economic responsibility for his wife and three children, he felt very guilty. Nevertheless, he made a decision to go forward and look for something he liked better.
>
> Over the course of the next three years, he wandered from job to job, but still did not hit on what he wanted. This threw his wife into a tizzy, because all the stability she and the family had grown used to seemed to be undermined. Even his mother and father said, "You're crazy!" Ned's guilt got worse.
>
> Seeking spiritual counseling, Ned began to consider their worries and fears just a reflection of his own. Instead of seeing them as an "attack" to his male-provider image, he saw them as mirroring his very own worries and fears that kept him chained to the factory job in the first place. His Inner Scarecrow (Mind) "clicked in", together with his Inner Tin Man (Heart), Inner Cowardly Lion (Will) and Inner Toto (Spirit), overruling the Fake Professor of guilt. Once he

absolutely made up his mind to go forward, asserting his Soul Power, he suddenly experienced God's Grace: through a strange coincidence, meeting someone he didn't know in the local diner, he "chanced" upon a major opportunity as a sales rep for a breakthrough new product.

Soon, Ned was making "a fortune", and loving it. And his wife, of course, was very happy he didn't listen to her fears, and followed his *Yellow Brick Road* through to completion.

When all seems most lost, and we get the most resistance, that's when we must be the most committed and most determined to assert our spiritual power and claim our right to the freedom of the *Oz State of Mind*. That's what throws the door open to our Inner Wizard:

*"Please don't cry anymore. I'll get you into see the Wizard somehow. I had an Auntie Em myself once,"* said the guard to the Wizard's chamber, eavesdropping on Dorothy's guilt-trip, while dripping mercifully with tears.

Then, with a boundless display of compassion from the guard, the massively imposing doors to the Wizard's "Holy of Holies" open: Our foursome, and Toto, enter.

With great dramatic fanfare, with ominous music in the background, we see our troop cautiously walking down the long tunnel to Oz's "altar", where the fantastic projection, all aflame with the Wizard's face, is addressing them.

The tunnel symbolizes that every Soul must go deeper and deeper into our subconscious and unconscious, until we surrender to very depths of our guilt and fears, so we can "Let go and Let God." Like our intrepid band of travelers, our Souls must shine a light on our worst terror, the face of raw, brutal, male power: *"Oz, the Great and Powerful."*

In the movie we see the Scarecrow, Lion, Dorothy, Tin Man, and finally Toto, all approaching the terrifying image of Oz. Like Ned, in the above anecdote, we stand possessed of our faculties, one-pointedly focused on our goals, despite the smoking-fears and the smoking-wrath of others around us. This is Pure Faith. It is unstoppable, even in the face of terror. That's when the Power of Grace opens up in our Life. Though our knees be knocking, victory is certain!

*"You dare to come to me for a heart, do you? You clinking, clanking, clattering, collection of caliginous junk?,"* scowled the Wizard to the Tin Man, who was clanking with fear. *"And you Scarecrow, have the effrontery to ask for a brain. You billowing bale of bovine fodder. And you Lion"* ... [he faints]... after which, Dorothy, ever on the side of the good, speaks her mind: *"You ought to be ashamed of yourself, frightening him like that when he came to you for help."*

*"Silence whipper-snapper,"* rebukes Oz, parentally. *"The Beneficent Oz has every intention of granting your requests."* At this point, everyone, including the dead-fainted Cowardly Lion, perks up. *"But...,"* coos the Wizard, *"first you must prove yourself worthy by performing a very small task: Bring me the broomstick of the Witch of the West."* No small task, as the Tin Man observes: *"But, if we do that, we'll have to kill her to get it..."*

*"Bring me the broomstick,"* fumes Oz more terrifyingly, *"and I'll grant your requests. Now go!"*

The broomstick of the Wicked Witch of the West? What does this mean? What is the spiritual meaning behind it?

The broomstick is the very symbol of the Witch's Power. It is that which propels her through the air, making her a fearful presence throughout Oz that can suddenly show up anywhere, just as our Witch-of-expansion can threaten our spiritual freedom, anywhere. By asking Dorothy to bring back the broomstick, the Great Oz is forcing Dorothy to gain the male knowledge she needs to get home. Indeed, the broomstick, phallic-like and inserted between the Witch's riding legs, is the symbol of the forceful, assertive, male-side that every Soul must own, to get home to his/her True Self.

Despite the smoke and mirrors, simply a reflection of our own fear of asserting our male power, our Inner Wizard is teaching us not to be afraid. He is forcing us to face our fear and go beyond it… to master its power! For a truly spiritually-committed Soul, there is no turning back. Faith requires you to bring back the broomstick. You must own all your power, completely, even the side of yourself of which you are most afraid. Dorothy, who sheepishly introduced herself to the Wizard as *"Dorothy, the small and meek,"* must throw off this pathetic Kansan fake humility.

She must now let out her powerful, assertive Light in the ultimate test of her personal power. Our Inner Wizard, our male-side – the necessary ruby-balance to our Inner Glinda, without which we cannot heal our

Soul – is forcing us to deny our weakness and our fears. Our Inner Wizard is forcing us to confront this Power in us and *"bring it back"* – to own it, totally forgive it, and be the Light we are. Without apologies to anyone!

This is what Oz requires before you can attain the *Oz State of Mind*: *"Bring back the broomstick of the Wicked Witch of the West."* Turn your evil self-betrayal – your denial of your powerful, spiritual Self – into Light. Put aside your mortal, Kansan doubts once and for all.

Now is your chance. Pass the test of your Inner Wizard.

Unseat the Witch. Ride her broomstick to your freedom. Take back your Power from her. If necessary, by force!

## Soul Lesson # 16:

## Surviving the Haunted Forest: Flying Monkeys

The power of the broomstick of the Wicked Witch of the West is really the Power of the *Oz State of Mind*, but in reverse polarity. Instead of using your spiritual power to create wondrous, exciting, uplifting experiences, you are using your spiritual power to create fearful, threatening, emotionally damaging experiences. The same creative spiritual power you use to create evil witches in your Life is the same spiritual power you use to create Glindas.

The more you follow your *Yellow Brick Road*, the more you clear out the old ghosts so your spiritual Light can shine, the more you will become aware of the deep connection between your "inner life" and your "outer life". You will become hauntingly aware that your feelings, thoughts, words, and actions are mirrored back to you. You will discover your Oz Power as a creative being, inwardly manufacturing your outer experiences in your Life, for good or bad. What you sow is what you reap. What you reap, you have previously sown. Indeed, there is not a single experience that comes to you on *The Yellow Brick Road* that is not, in some fashion, a mirror of one of the following:

1. A mirror of some desire you have, or a complex of many desires, strung together.

2. A mirror of some kind of belief you have.

3. A mirror of some kind of group belief, or historical current, in which you participate.

4. Sub- or unconscious thought patterns, desires, or choices of which you are unaware, but nonetheless are determining your outer experiences.

5. Shared human life experiences/beliefs, such as illness or death.

6. Shared human sense experiences, such as smells, feelings, color perceptions, touch, etc. programmed into the body's mechanism.

7. Understandings, be they scientific, personal or religious – which become accepted truths, even if incomplete or false.

8. Some kind of thought, word, or deed you directed towards another, now returning back to you, a mirror of yourself.

Some combination of these – indeed, thousands or millions of these eight basics – form the "software" by which our Mind, Heart and Will are programmed, and which shape our experiences in Life, including the experience of the entire world which humans share.

> Take a moment. Just look at your personal life and what you are experiencing outwardly. Now try to back-track the experiences to your inner thought life, and you'll see how true this list is.

> Go further now. Look at the current events in the newspaper and try to back-track these to the "inner lives" of the people and nations creating the news. You may be shocked to realize, we are creating our own hells, personally and politically, simply by how we are programmed to function.

All our problems are the result of negative attitudes or thinking. Like Dorothy, when we have not completely melted our inner problems – our guilt, for example – they will manifest as living problems in our outer reality. They will manifest not just as thoughts or feelings, but also as concrete events and experiences. These experiences will be as frightening as we believe our problems to actually be. They mirror our fright so we can face it, supersede it, and grow spiritually. There is no fear that must be put before our expansion towards God, for that would turn fear into an idol, and therefore an obstruction to our spiritual ascent.

So, like our intrepid band of travelers, we must all be brave enough to enter our *Haunted Forest*. We must all be strong enough to face our *shadow*, as the psychologist Carl Jung termed it. All the haunting ghosts in our lives must be dispelled from our Inner Selves. No one can prepare for bringing back the broomstick, unless one is willing to face the ghosts that are underneath our fear of power. No one gains male-wisdom, receiving access to their Inner Wizard, until they shirk their timidity, brave their hauntings, and triumph:

> Belinda grew up poverty stricken. One day she hit the lottery and made $ 500,000. But, one year later, because of supposedly bad investment counseling, she found herself right back where she was. The problem was not the advice.
>
> The problem was she had not undone her programming that was creating the inner reality of poverty. It took 3 years of undoing her programming around money – which went back three generations of impoverished immigrants – but eventually, program changed, Belinda's ghosts vanished. She's now making six figures.
>
> Fred, by his own admission, was a womanizer. One day, he met a lady, seemingly pure and innocent, that absolutely knocked his socks off. He married her, with the sincerest desires in his heart. However, he was shocked when, six months into the marriage, it turned out that his wife's history was no less sordid than Fred's. Before Fred could blink, his wife returned to him everything that he had done to other women. He suddenly woke up and sought some spiritual counseling.
>
> Fred did not even remember it consciously, and it only came up in hypnosis, but his father had the exact same womanizing patterns he had,

despite his supposedly successful marriage to Fred's mom. Fred had been unconsciously haunted by his father his whole life but didn't know it.

In the movie, as our travelers enter their Haunted Forest, they are greeted by a foreboding sign: *"Haunted Forest. I'd turn back if I were you."* This is how we can all feel at first, when *The Yellow Brick Road* brings us an experience of facing our shadows. We, like the Cowardly Lion in the movie, might want to run away from what's haunting us. However, mustering the shared conviction of Mind and Heart, it is up to our Inner Scarecrow and Inner Tin Man to stop our Cowardly Lion from retreating, as they quickly do.

At the entrance of the forest, we see two wise owls with eyes aglow. They are reminders that by going forward to face our ghosts, we will achieve the vision of Wizard Wisdom needed to own the Witch's broomstick. But, to get such Wisdom, we must also face our own self-blame and inner attacks; thus, after the owls, we see two attack-birds, buzzards, also with glowing eyes.

*"I believe there's spooks around here,"* says the Scarecrow. *"Don't you believe in spooks?,"* says the Cowardly Lion to the Tin Man. *"That's ridiculous! Spooks. That's silly!,"* at which point the Tin Man levitates upward and comes crashing down.

*"I do believe in spooks. I do believe in spooks. I do. I do. I do. I do...,"* chants the Cowardly Lion to avoid a similar poltergeist attack. This is precisely how we create our shadow experiences: believing in spooks. We believe in

our guilt. We believe in our phobia. We believe that we are still haunted by family scripts and are still scarred by our parents – and then, by believing these to be real, we make them real and keep them real. We take these beliefs into our inner psychic programming and then manufacture our outer experiences accordingly.

Our Inner Cowardly Lion, by believing in spooks, actually creates spooks in our lives or intensifies them. Owning our broomstick begins with *disbelieving* our spooks. Disbelieving our spooks, and neutralizing their hold over us, is the first step towards re-programming ourselves and taking back our Power.

Witnessing their turmoil within her crystal ball and deciding to prey upon it, the Wicked Witch sets out with a vengeance: *"Take your army to the Haunted Forest and bring me that girl and the dog. Do what you like with the others."*

The Witch, representing the shadow-self that our travelers need to master, sends out the entire army of Flying Monkeys to attack and kidnap Dorothy and Toto. Part of her strategy is to separate our soul from our Mind, Heart, and Will, so we have no defenses, and can fall under the mind, heart, and will of the Wicked Witch, a common strategy amongst political dictators, demagogues, cult-leaders and deranged psychotherapists.

In Hindu mythology, the Flying Monkey is the demigod *Hanuman*, as it also is in Chinese Buddhist mythology. Hanuman is a trickster, who is always playing jokes. When we start to disbelieve our spooks and deny their haunting control over our lives, it is not uncommon to experience these tricksters.

The decision, made in faith, to *disbelieve our spooks*, sets in motion a kind of "antivirus" within our psychic apparatus. It immediately begins to undo our very deep programming. Unfortunately, there is a side of us that has grown dependent on our previous programming. That side of us can send up all sorts of Inner Flying Monkeys that can attack us. We may feel waves of panic, disorientation, self-doubt, fractured thoughts, floods of rationalizations, flying around in our mind and feelings. The side of you that wants to change is suddenly assaulted by the side of you that doesn't want to change, which seems to be defending its turf. This side of you which resists change, casts the trickster Flying Monkeys to the sky to capture you. Traditional religions might consider these Flying Monkeys "satanic", like the Serpent in the Garden of Eden who tricked Adam and Eve.

Flying Monkeys are usually unavoidable when we are taking a step towards de-programming ourselves on such a deep, threatening level. They rarely appear if you are working on the surface of your consciousness; they only appear if you are penetrating below the surface to your subconscious or unconscious, where your obstructive mirrors are deeply lodged.

However, Flying Monkeys themselves are nothing to fear at all. The more they attack, the more adamant and determined you should become. Then, with each layer of your programming that you peel off, more and more of their wings are clipped, until, with your new programming installed, you feel more anchored than ever in the *Oz State of Mind,* your house free from haunts.

Braving the Haunted Forest is not something you should do initially by yourself. Begin always with a very qualified, experienced counselor who has actually done the work on him or herself. Don't just go by their degrees or diplomas; this is very intense spiritual work and real experience is the only real qualification.

However, there is no serious spiritual traveler who can avoid spending time, and maybe a little money, going through their Haunted Forest.

Face your ghosts with determination. Face them, if you can, with a sense of humor. Exorcise their haunting of your Mind, Heart and Will.

So, even if the Flying Monkeys cart your Soul (Dorothy) and Spirit (Toto) off to the Witch's Castle, your Mind (Inner Scarecrow), your Heart (Tin Man), and your Will (Cowardly Lion), will quickly rebound and come to your rescue. You will be "saved" as some religions call it. You will be made Whole!

# Soul Lesson # 17:

# Melting your Wicked Witch

Because working through our darkest haunts can be terrifying, we may sometimes be tempted to give into the Witch. We might, like Dorothy, be tempted to lose our ruby-balance, giving away our slippers, abandoning our spiritual goals.

But it is important to understand, from a spiritual perspective, that this is not possible: Your Spirit is, by its very Nature, indomitable, born of the Creator. It is Pure Spiritual Consciousness, a "ray" of Divine Energy. Even if you do weaken, momentarily, you really cannot lose completely: Your own indomitable (Toto-barking) Spirit, under the direction of your Soul, will never let you forfeit or lose, no matter how long or difficult the journey. It must always, by its Sacred Nature, stay true to itself, Glinda-compassed.

Thus, the moment the Witch tries to forcibly take Dorothy's ruby slippers, her crooked, arthritic, sickly, green fingers receive the shock of their life: Dorothy's own spiritual force leaps out from the shoes and stings her, so much so, that the Witch must now plan Dorothy's murder – the very extinction of her Living Soul – in order to get the shoes.

Your shadow-self is very, very deep. It's not easy to stop the Witch. She will continue to threaten you, until you master her power and own her broomstick. She will turn an hourglass over, barricade you in a dungeon, make you face your shadow-self with naked, fleshly, mortal vulnerability. She is, once again, actually a friend-in-disguise, helping you to grow, reflecting your own worst mortal fears back to yourself, so you can become aware of them, overcome your Inner Cowardly Lion, and take back your Power.

No sooner does the Witch imprison Dorothy, that Dorothy plummets even deeper into her guilt, in order to face it more squarely and regain the Power to free herself. Auntie Em appears in the Witch's crystal ball, *"Dorothy. Dorothy. Where are you? Please. It's Auntie Em. We're trying to find you."* Dorothy tries to communicate with Auntie Em, but having not yet finished clearing her guilt, Auntie Em's sweet face dissolves indistinguishably into the scowling face of the Wicked Witch. Dorothy's guilt towards Auntie Em *is* the Wicked Witch! She cannot be free of the latter, until she is free of the former.

Imprisoned bodily in the Witch's castle, with the hourglass leaking away, all seems hopeless for Dorothy, who must now face her guilt to the point of confronting her own spiritual death. If she hadn't left Kansas,

Dorothy would have experienced a spiritual death. Now, she must experience that fear of death in order to be free of the guilt from having left Kansas. This is the "mind game" that our Inner Flying Monkeys are always tricking us to play when we judge ourselves, unfairly, for simply daring to be ourselves.

Staring terror directly in the face, with tears streaming down, we see our heroine finally undergoing a complete, unabashed, surrender. Losing her last defense, Dorothy now abandons herself completely to her fear, guilt, and hopelessness. Before us, we see someone seemingly broken, nullified, forsaken, and emptied-of-possibility. Dorothy has surrendered to the point of complete "death".

This is the spiritual "turning point" of our Soul. This is the spiritual turning point that we have been moving towards from the very moment our Witch-of-expansion challenged us by skywriting *"Surrender Dorothy,"* high above the Emerald City. This is the greatest low before the upward turn, the night before the dawn, the "no place to go but up". Indeed, when your surrender is complete and you've given UP to God – surrendering your life completely to the Divine Purpose – it's just then, that Light always breaks through:

Toto, our irrepressible Spirit, leaps over the castle moat, scampering over rocks and mini-mountains, until he finds the Scarecrow, the Tin Man, and the Lion. Your feisty Spirit begins to shine through the shadow of your Inner Witch. The Light of your undaunted True Self begins to shine. *"Can't you see?,"* observes the supposedly brainless Scarecrow, *"He's come to take us to Dorothy."*

Declaring the freedom of our Soul, to the point of complete surrender, causes an amazing turnaround: The Tin Man, supposedly heartless, begins to weep with compassion for Dorothy's imprisonment. The Scarecrow, hardly dumb at all, thinks up an ingenious plan to save her. The supposedly Cowardly Lion finds a burst of fortitude to breach the castle's walls, putting his own petty vital fears aside.

From spiritual death is released "hope," "faith," "resurrection," "new birth," and "transcendence" – all the qualities that are at the core of all the world's greatest faiths. Your Inner Scarecrow, Inner Tin Man, and Inner Lion, led by your Toto-Spirit, invade the *Witch's Castle*, symbolizing her *stronghold* over our Soul. Like the Tin Man's ax, the loving power of Pure Love smashes through the bolted door and blows it open. Our Soul is set free. We escape.

But the Witch of the West, ever trying to prevent our spiritual expansion, will continue to try to trap us. Her armies of minions will hunt after us. Eventually, we will get cornered. We will have the Witch on one side of us and her minions on the other side of us. Caught like a rat between two equally lethal alternatives, Our Mind will burn with fear; our Witch will try to set our Inner Scarecrow in flames, turning the spiritual flame of our Mind against us.

However, the Witch cannot win, ever. She is only a shadow upon our Light. It is, in fact, our Light that forms her shadow nature. We gave her power by *be-*

*lieving* that we were 100% responsible for the conditions in Kansas. We gave her power by denying ourselves and not living by the true dictates of our Soul. We gave the Witch power by feeling guilty and not treating ourselves compassionately.

Realizing this ancient spiritual truth, a miracle now takes place: Our Inner Dorothy, our Soul, grabs a bucket of water to extinguish the flames of self-attacking guilt and fear, in order to save our Inner Scarecrow from the Witch's tirade and torment. Hurling the water at the Scarecrow, it hits the Witch right in her menacing face:

*"Look what you've done,"* screams the Witch. *"I'm melting... melting. Oh what a world. What a world. Who would have thought a good little girl like you could destroy my beautiful wickedness."*

Dorothy looks on compassionately, her own guilt and self-hatred melting with the Witch. Nevertheless, Dorothy herself had taken the initiative to extinguish her Witch. She has discovered her own Power! She is no longer the victim!

*Water*, the symbol of *Living Spirit* and *Total Forgiveness*, has come to Dorothy's rescue. Water, whose atomic weight is "18", the *Kabbalistic* numerological equivalent for the Power of *Life*, has melted Dorothy's guilt and fear. Water – which represents in many mythologies *The Purified Unconscious, God's Own Mind or Being*, the oceanic *Womb of Life* – has melted away all the negative experiences of the Witch's Castle. The nightmare is over. The materialization of Dorothy's deepest fears has melted… melted… surrendered completely into nothingness.

Our Soul, after truly facing its darkest shadow and staring it right in the face, is always set free. *"The Truth will set you free."* We all triumph, if we are willing to do the difficult emotional and psychological work and go through our programs and sins, consciously exposing them to the Light of Love and Divine Forgiveness. This is the essence of "repentance" or "therapy" or "self-purification", *The Yellow Brick Road* that is our human spiritual adventure on earth.

As the Witch melts, the self-doubt of our Inner Scarecrow melts: "I'm not stupid. I knew Kansas was a dead end. Why should I deny my intelligence for deciding to be different?" As the Witch melts, the cowardice of our Inner Lion also melts: "It took courage to leave Kansas; I'm proud of myself. Otherwise, I would have stayed in pig muck for the rest of my life." As the Witch melts, the self-doubt of our Inner Tin Man also melts: "There was no reason for my heart to be so missing towards myself; I was just a person who needed to be free; it's my right. I didn't mean to hurt Auntie Em, but I'm only human."

And lastly – as the Witch melts – Toto just continues to bark, defiantly, as he has done throughout the movie. Nothing, absolutely nothing, can stop your Spirit from expressing its True Nature. Each bark by Toto is an affirmation of our innate spiritual greatness:

*"Hail to Dorothy. The Wicked Witch is dead,"* says the guard. *"Hail, hail to Dorothy,"* we hear the entire troop of guards echo. Those who were controlled by the

Witch now celebrate along with Dorothy. It is they who hand her the Witch's broomstick. Our Inner psychological guards or defenses that once prevented us from killing our Inner Witch now become our allies. Our fears are now fully recognized by us as friends.

Facing the Witch with fortitude and forgiveness, we have taken back the Witch's power as our own. We melted her by Love of our Self, in perfect coordination with our Mind, Heart, Will and Spirit. We are now a whole Human Soul, equally possessed of our female, and now our male, powers.

Now, we are ready to receive the gift of our Wizard Wisdom.

# Soul Lesson # 18:

## Revealing Your Inner Wizard

The broomstick, the very Power of the Witch you feared, is more forceful than all your relationships, family, friends, society and the world. It represents the Light of your male-side, which refuses to be held back or contained. Now, it is firmly in your hand!

Together with your cohorts, you have come to the Wizard to claim your prize: *The Wisdom of your Inner Wizard.* Indeed, throughout the story, Dorothy is dressed in a blue frock: Blue is the color of Wisdom, of the 5th or throat *chakra* in the Hindu metaphysical system. Blue is the power of "externalized mind": conscious thoughts which shape your chosen destiny and purpose. This corresponds to *daat* in *Kabbalistic* system or the "Word" made flesh in Christology.

*"Can I believe my eyes? Why have you come back?,"* fumes the Wizard. *"Please sir,"* responds Dorothy, *"We've done*

*what you told us. We brought you the broomstick of the Wicked Witch of the West. We melted her." "Ahh... you liquidated her. Very resourceful,"* puns the Wizard, thanks to the genius of the Hollywood scriptwriter.

Dorothy and her cohorts then ask the Wizard to honor his promise, but… to their great dismay… the Wizard balks. Attempting to buy time (since he never imagined Dorothy could have succeeded in melting the Witch,) he orders them: *"Come back tomorrow."*

But now, the Wizard's scare tactics do not work; Dorothy is too strong. She has braved her darkest fears, fully surrendered to them all, and turned them from darkness to light. She fears no one anymore; her male-side is so powerful, she will even challenge the Great Oz: *"Tomorrow? But I want to go home now. If you were really great and powerful, you'd keep your promises."*

At the moment that Dorothy puts her foot down, asserting her Self even in the face of the Wizard's histrionics, we see Toto, of course, representing her Spirit, drawing back the curtain. There, we see a feeble, white-haired man, frantically pulling levers, attempting to cover up his fraud, beginning to panic: *"Pay no attention to that man behind the curtain."* The Wizard has been unmasked; he's been revealed as a *"humbug."* *"You're a very bad man,"* Dorothy accuses, realizing the sham. But, the Wizard responds with the naked truth: *"Oh no my dear, I'm a very good man. I'm just a very bad Wizard."* Indeed!

For days on end, Dorothy has been on a search for the Inner Wisdom necessary to arrive home, but now, she realizes *"The "Wonderful Wizard of Oz"* is not a *"whiz-of-*

*a-whiz, if ever a whiz-there-was"*, but a mere mortal human being.

Dorothy thought the power was in the Wizard, but the Wizard was, no less than the Witch, powerless. As long as our Souls believe we are powerless, we magically project our belief upon the Wizard, thinking he alone has the power to deliver us, when it is really *our* Power that we are seeking.

We all, when we set out on a spiritual path, create a powerful goal, god, or vision, in our minds and hearts. We may believe there is a powerful, austere "God" – some distant, wrathful "Other" that must be propitiated, whose sacrifices must be fulfilled, whose tasks, like bringing back the broom, must be accomplished before we can receive "His" anointing.

Such a belief is often psychologically critical when you first enter upon your *Yellow Brick Road.* That's because unless you believe, innocently, in the possibility or the potential for change, i.e. a Higher Vision or "God", you cannot easily find the strength to defy the Kansan world and seek the *Oz State of Mind*. God, for many of us, when we first begin our *Yellow Brick Road*, often serves us like a kind of "device", like the Wizard's machinery, by which we strengthen our True Egos and begin our spiritual ascent to Oz, inspite of resistance or even threats from others.

However, after we reach the point of owning our own Power, our view of God changes. Stronger, more psychologically individuated, we no longer relate to God as most people do, as a great "super-ego", a controlling, demanding Parental Other upon whom our fate depends, like the smoke-bellowing Wizard. We begin to realize that there is no smoking, demanding, parental-like Wizard controlling us. Instead, you begin to realize that the Power of the Wizard appearing outside you – like all the characters Dorothy has met – is a Power that's there right alongside of you, if not inside you, all along. You and God are a Living Relationship, a covenantal miracle. God's Power and Yours are different in scale of Mind, Heart and Will – God creates universes, you create "things" – but it is one and the same Essential Power.

Indeed, Dorothy was given that hint continuously upon her arrival in the Emerald City: She saw the face of the Wizard in the doorman, the driver of the "horse of a different color", in the compassionate guard who protects the enclave of the Wizard, and of course, in the face of Professor Marvel, back on Kansas. The face of the Wisdom we are seeking is always there all around us, present in the ordinary faces of the many "ordinary" people who are helping us on Life's journey.

Our Wizard has been unmasked to reveal another *wizard* (lower case), truer, more humbly human – and, ironically, a much, much more powerful one. Each and every one of us has this Inner Wizard. Each and every one of us mortals contains the Power to bring us home to our True Selves. God is not just outside us, but inside us. The *Inner* Chamber of the Wizard, which originally terrifies us until we own our broomstick, is really our own Inner Self. God's Spirit, which is parceled off as our own Soul, is the very Power we have been seeking, and, in fact, the Only Power there is:

Look at any problem you have with people in your Life, regardless of what they are doing "to you" and see them as God's Light. See them as God's Wisdom. See them as Mortal Wizards.

See them as Love. See them as God's Spirit in individual form, playing a role in your personal script to help you grow and expand spiritually. Some play the role of anger; others play the role of jealousy, or hatred. Others play the role of passion. All play the role of teacher.

**Everyone is a human form of the same Spirit. We are all One.** *This is the first lesson of our Inner Wizard.*

Our Inner Wizard teaches us the mystical secret of the ages: *The Power of God is in us.* We, mortal we, just the way we are, are the Wizard we've been seeking. Implanted within us is all the Wisdom we need, God's Very Own Presence. All we have to do is let it out and release the Divine Potential that's been implanted within us, sharing this with the Divine Potential also released by others. Our Toto-Spirit must pull aside the curtain for all of us. Only then can we discover the Hidden Power of our human natures, the Inner Wizard that lies within each and every mortal being.

Yes, even though our Wizard has been defrocked, he, and we, still possess great Godly gifts of understanding and discernment. Turning to the supposedly brainless Scarecrow, he bestows upon him a diploma, a Ph.D., *"a doctor of thinkology"*. Immediately the Scarecrow rattles off Euclid's formula for the relationship between the sides of a right triangle. Turning to our

Cowardly Lion, he bestows upon him a medal, declaring him to be a bonafide member of the *"Legion of Courage."* Finally, turning to the Tin Man, he bestows upon him a *"testimonial"*, a ticking heart, to celebrate his great depths of compassion as a *"ph... ph... good deed do-er,"* i.e. a philanthropist.

Your Soul was created perfectly by a Perfect Creator. Your Mind has always been brilliant. Your Heart has always been strong and compassionate. Your Will has always been courageous. Even through your stupidity, your empty feelings, and your cowardice, you have been expressing the Power within you – but through the eyes of self-doubt, self-criticism, even self-hatred, rather than through the eyes of Self Love.

> **See yourself always with Self Love, and you will realize that you are not lacking anything, nor is your Inner Scarecrow, Inner Tin Man or Inner Lion.**
>
> *This is the second lesson of our Inner Wizard.*

The Wizard did not give the Scarecrow some brains, the Tin Man a heart or the Lion some courage; they had *already displayed* these on *The Yellow Brick Road* and in braving the Witch's stronghold. The Wizard simply demonstrated Wisdom: teaching them Self Love, he *validated* the brains, the heart, and the courage they already had, but which, in their self-criticism, they had become too blind to see.

> Reverse the curse. See your personal pain and suffering as diplomas, clocks and medals. Believe this to be true, in faith. Start out fresh. Let

your curses become turned into blessings. It is only your self-hatred that withholds your spiritual Power from you.

**Belief in your Self – your True Self, born directly from God – is the start of all Wisdom.** *This is the third lesson of our Inner Wizard.*

Alas, Dorothy is not like her three cohorts. They are not human. She is. The Mind is satisfied with learning; the Heart is satisfied with feeling; the Will is satisfied by courage or faith. But, the human being, *Made in the Image and Likeness of God,* is more complex, a Whole which is greater than the sum of its parts. So, mastering a more complete Power of God-within, is considerably more complicated. Alas, as Dorothy sadly recognizes, there is nothing in the Wizard's bag-of-tricks that can get a Human Soul – comprised of Mind, Heart, Will *and* a Toto-Spirit – back home. Something more dramatic is necessary.

*"You've forced me into a cataclysmic decision,"* declares the Wizard. The former balloonist, coincidentally from the great state of Kansas, who had landed in Oz and was declared *"Wizard Deluxe",* now promises, with great bombast, to bring Dorothy back home himself. Dorothy, the Wizard and Toto will share his hot air balloon, and together, they will descend back to *"The Land of E Pluribus Unum"* together. Dorothy is thrilled.

But, as millions upon millions of viewers see, every year, the all-too-mortal Wizard, however spiritually-insightful and well-intentioned, will fail. His promise will turn out to be, like his balloon, a bag of "hot air."

Can you guess why? Can you guess the final spiritual lesson of our Inner Wizard?

## Soul Lesson #19:

## Escaped Balloons: Know Yourself.

It's the climax of movie and Dorothy's spiritual adventure. There stands the balloon that carried the so-called "wizard" to Oz in the first place, obviously launched from the Omaha State Fair. There too stands the Wizard, looking all too mortal with top hat in hand, and Dorothy and Toto along with him in the balloon basket.

However mortal in appearance though, our Wizard just can't let down his guard: the sham he fell into when he descended into Oz continues. With tremendous force of false ego – like the balloon swollen with "hot air" – he talks about his *"technically unexplainable journey into the outer stratosphere ... to confer, converse and otherwise hobnob with my brother wizards."*

Then, continuing his regal bombast, he appoints the Scarecrow, *"by virtue of his highly superior brains"* to rule in his stead, *"assisted by the Tin Man, by virtue of his magnificent heart, and the Lion, by virtue of his courage."* There is great spiritual Wisdom to these pronouncements. Just as Dorothy first met the Scarecrow, then second, met the Tin Man, and third, met the Lion, the Wizard here affirms the same exact priority.

Whether in the personal sphere of governing an individual life, or in the larger sphere of governing a society, the priority – Scarecrow, Tin Man and Lion – is critical. No realm, whether individual or collective, can be governed effectively without all three properly weighted. Mind must be assisted by Heart and Courage, in that order. Mind, assisted by Heart and Courage, in perfect harmony, safeguards the peace, wellbeing, purpose and needs of every individual and all human life.

But when Mind is not assisted by Heart, and Courage acts anyway, we get idiotic wars and stupid belligerent policies. When Heart rules, and Mind is dormant, but Courage acts, you get powerful displays of emotionalism that are ineffectual, sentimental and lacking vision. When Mind and Heart are allied, but there is no Courage, there is excessive traditionalism and stagnation. Every single political problem we have in the world is due to an imbalance of the Scarecrow, Tin Man and Lion, as spiritual factors within every government or its populace. Every single problem Dorothy has had, or we have, is due to a similar imbalance.

As for our Wizard, although he has a healthy supply of Mind, (and thus, he was pronounced a Wizard upon landing in Oz) and some compassion, (offering to take Dorothy home,) he severely lacks courage. He is deceitful to a fault, and more concerned about his appearance to others than being brave enough to tell the truth. So, it is not surprising, that with all his false ego, being so "puffed up" with false pride, his balloon just sails away uncontrollably. *"I can't come back. I don't know how it works."*

Toto, representing Dorothy's Spirit, would never permit her to sail away under the pretense of false ego, for it has been his task down *The Yellow Brick Road* to continuously guard her spiritual journey. It is Toto that causes the balloon to escape as a gift to her. His fire is aroused by the sight of a cat, which in ancient Egypt, represents a higher spiritual power. This is an indication that Dorothy needed to receive some Higher Knowledge. Toto lunges out of the basket. Dorothy quickly chases after him. The final mirror of Dorothy's false ego, the false, hat-waving Wizard, flies away. Dorothy is poised for the all-important final lesson from her Inner Wizard.

Heartbroken, and appearing to lose faith, Dorothy becomes worried she will never go home. No longer plagued with guilt, she is now plagued by grief: *"Auntie Em must have stopped wondering what happened to me by now."*

Nevertheless, this too, is a gift: Grief is always the emotion that appears when we are about to make the final reconciliation in ourselves. Grief signals our readiness to finally let go of our mistakes, our self-blame, our blaming of others, and the hurt we think we caused. Grief signals the end of our *Yellow Brick Road* of forgiveness. There is little left to forgive any more. The past is passed. We are ready to be *alive*, fully alive, in the *present:* the *Presence* that is God.

Just as Dorothy seems to be losing direction, not knowing where to go, we see a glowing, pink bubble descending into the plaza: Glinda, the Good Witch of the North, has come to be her compass, once again, pointing in the direction of "magnetic north" – UP in her spiritual ascent.

*"Will you help me? Can you help me?,"* pleads Dorothy to Glinda. *"You don't need to be helped by anyone anymore. You've always had the Power to go back to Kansas,"* replies Glinda assuredly. *"I have?,"* asks Dorothy, surprised. *"Then why didn't you tell her before?,"* said the Scarecrow. *"Because,"* replied Glinda all-knowingly, *"She wouldn't have believed me. She had to learn it for herself."*

*"What have you learned, Dorothy?,"* queries the Tin Man:

> *"I think it wasn't enough to want to see Uncle Henry and Auntie Em. And it's that if I ever go looking for my heart's desire again, I won't look any further than my own backyard. Because if it isn't there, I never really lost it to begin with."*

**You are given everything you need in Life, the correct parents, the correct Life circumstances, the correct balance of resources and gifts – you need only *see* it that way. That's Heaven!**

> *Yes, this is the fourth and last lesson of our Inner Wizard!*

All along, Dorothy was believing in fake Wizards, Witches, Munchkins, a Scarecrow, a Tin Man, and a Cowardly Lion. But, to believe in some other mere mortal over yourself, to deny your own self-knowledge and trust another's instead? Never!

That was the final lesson of false ego delivered by our Inner Wizard. That was the mistake Dorothy made in Kansas before she began her journey: Trusting others over her Self, to the *denial* of her Self. It's a lesson she learned the hard way. It's a lesson, we must all learn, any way we can.

When we finally learn to trust our True Selves – not to disparage or ignore others, but to honor them as they are, but in their correct place – that's when we finally, like Dorothy, reach spiritual enlightenment. That's when our Witch-of-expansion finally gets back her sister's ruby slippers. That's when our reckless drive for freedom becomes balanced with relationships to others. That's when we can return to our simple, humble, sometimes humdrum, Kansan life – poised and ruby-balanced – so we no longer need to kill the Witch-of-contraction to set ourselves free.

When we finally learn to trust our True Selves, we no longer have to forfeit psychological balance and a healthy home-life to open up our spiritual imagination and creative potential. Black & white actuality no longer limits *Technicolor* possibility. We finally – in a true spiritual sense, not in a false Kansan sense – *grow up!* We become adults, but, without the *adult-eration*.

As the false ego of the fake Wizard, in whom we had placed our false hopes, sails away unanchored, Dorothy permanently anchors the *Oz State of Mind*. That State of Consciousness you have been seeking, the path to Perfect Grace, the path to happiness and spiritual integrity has *never been* outside you. It's been right where we all forget to look for it: right in our own backyard. Now the Witch-of-expansion and the Witch-of-contraction fuse into one Good Witch! Everything is now compassed UP!

Hearing the correctness of this self-understanding, Glinda reminds us all of our Power: *"Now those magic slippers will take you home in two seconds."* *"Toto too?,"* asks Dorothy. *"Toto too,"* responds Glinda. Dorothy's Spirit will never be taken from her again!

> The Power has always been ours;
> we only needed to look within.

# Soul Lesson #20 (actually, ∞): There's No Place Like Home

Clicking the heels of her ruby slippers together, Dorothy propels her way home. There is no struggle, no confusion, no tumultuous whirlwind. She sails home guided by the Power of her thoughts: *"There's no place like home. There's no place like home. There's no place like home."* Dorothy has discovered the Pure Creativity of the *Oz State of Mind*. With innocent, Munchkin-like faith, with the clear-compassed certainty of her free will, she powers her way home on the wings of a prayer.

The heels, which are the *posterior* part of her slippers, representing the *past* learning from her journey to Oz, come together. The right and left sides, representing the Powers of both her Inner Wizard and her Inner Glinda, her male and female knowledge – a single God-Self – now click together with perfect ruby-balance.

Dorothy is no longer a divided Soul, shredded between the polar opposites of her mind – male/female, good witch/bad witch, *yin/yang*. Dorothy is now a single, integrated Human Soul. The outward spiraling cyclone of her disturbed Kansan mind, which had launched her *Somewhere Over the Rainbow,* now reverses itself in the movie, spiraling more and more inward, centripetally rather than centrifugally… until Dorothy lands home back in bed. It seemed like a dream. But, was it?

The spiritual lesson, which is the driving force of this great story's teachings, is this: No matter where you start off from, no matter how humble your beginnings, no matter how difficult, or even brutal the circumstances of your birth or life – within each and every person, situation, and event is a *gift*. Within it all, whether good witch or bad witch, is a *meaning*, a Spiritual Understanding and Knowledge which comes to you directly from God. It is the meaning of your purpose here in "Kansas," i.e., on earth.

Everything you experience in Life – from the moment you are born, till the moment you die – is designed as a vehicle, by a mutual agreement between you and God, through which you will discover the Hidden Powers of Spirit that have been housed within. Whether your experiences appear good or bad, it is all Good in purpose. It's all designed for the purpose of your spiritual growth, for your increasing awareness that the Supreme Power called "God" resides not just outwardly in the universe upon universe, but also within you, as your very True Spiritual Self.

So, reflected in the industrious face of Auntie Em, Dorothy now sees herself. She sees her own possessive love for her home. Now, in the face of Uncle Henry, dutifully managing the farm, Dorothy sees her own need for security. In Hunk, Hickory and Zeke, Dorothy sees her own Mind, Heart and Will, not always agreeing in the past, but all three her friends and allies.

In Professor Marvel, Dorothy can now see her own *truthful-falseness* – dreaming to be more than she was, so she could escape, separating from other people's control over her life, only to discover the deep connectedness, the Divine Love that was there all along.

Dorothy's heart opens and she wells up with this Divine Love – love for herself, and, love for others. The conflict which drove her from Kansas in the first place has been healed. She has arrived back in a *new-old* Kansas. Kansas has become transformed because *she* has become transformed. Dorothy has discovered the perfect Goodness of Life. She has changed her mind. She now sees things through the *Oz State of Mind*. She realizes the Perfect Grace that established her in the barnyard.

She even realizes the gift of Elvira Gulch, whose cruelty forced our Dorothy-Soul to face her Spirit and seek Higher Knowledge. There are no good witches, or bad, anymore. There is just Love, the Perfect Love of God expressing perfectly in the life that she had been granted. Dorothy, as a Soul, is now *awake*!

Are you awake? Have you woken up to the meaning of each and every person in your life? Have you woken up to their message, purpose, symbolic presence? Have you woken up from your dream that you are cursed in Kansas, born to suffer? Have you woken up from your belief that the world is divided, when, in fact, it is *you* that is divided (along with a lot of other people) – between Mind, Heart, Will, and Spirit?

Over the faces of each of her family members and friends, our awakened Dorothy now sees, superimposed, the learning and understanding which she gained by ascending to a Higher Oz Awareness. Are you awake? Do you see this when you look at your loved ones?

Each one of these people are from Kansas, but now, seen through Dorothy's new vision, they're also from Oz. Indeed now, the two states-of-minds have fused. When your *Oz State of (Extraordinary) Mind* and your *Kansan State of (Ordinary) Mind* have merged, when your Higher Universal Vision of Self and your earthly, mortal self become one, what results is the goal of all our dreams, philosophies, religions and spiritual disciplines: The realization of *God-Within*, the *"Kingdom,"* the *Messianic-Self*, the *Buddha*. There are many, many names for a similar human spiritual experience.

This realization is the exquisite Self-understanding that our earthly, fleshly, existence is a magnificent dance of God. It appears sometimes like pain, sometimes like pleasure, sometimes like good, sometimes like bad. But, in spite of appearances, the dance always reflects an Absolute Goodness, a Perfection which mirrors The Perfect One: God. This is what it means spiritually to *return home*.

*To return home* like Dorothy, is to understand that everything and everyone is Perfect, even with their imperfections. And yet, through our choices, utilizing the creative gift of free will, everything remains to be perfected in-the-flesh, made perfect materially, *"on earth, as it is in heaven."*

*"There is no place like home!,"* that is, our *True* Home! Although it appears as if we're living on earth, we have never really left our *True* Home. Our Souls are always one with God; we've just learned to believe they weren't, caught in a Kansan cyclone of confusion.

The final Soul Lesson that Dorothy and her cohorts give us, rings out to our Minds, Hearts, and Wills – a clear-sounding bell of spiritual triumph, the yap-yapping of our Toto-Spirit:

>You are a Living Soul.
>You are born of *THE* Living Soul, God.

In this Life, you must make a difficult journey down your *Yellow Brick Road*; it is necessary spiritual education. Down your *Yellow Brick Road*, you will learn about Life. Down your *Yellow Brick Road*, you will uncover your true spiritual nature as a human being. Down your *Yellow Brick Road* you will rise above this cyclone-torn world of colliding opposites. Down your *Yellow Brick Road* you will discover *"Somewhere Over the Rainbow, Way UP High!"*

But, everything you learn will be the exact same lesson in disguise:

>*Love.* That's the only lesson there is.
>All is love. Love is home!

So, in the final analysis, Oz is not different from Kansas. Kansas is not different from Oz. The difference was that before starting on *The Yellow Brick Road*, we looked at the humdrum earthly life around us and were blind to its beauty and its profound spiritual meaning. But now, we look out onto the boring, gray plane of Kansas and see a rainbow over the pigsty. In the faces of so many around us, we can see the Presence of God.

The Kansans? Well, they haven't changed much. They are still lost in their little world. They are still controlling and petty. They still get stuck in the mud. They still live a life that is without spiritual imagination and get tangled in their underwear – moaning about how awful life is, counting every penny as if it were a drop of blood. Through our spiritual journey, we did not change them. Alas, that is their responsibility; we can't do it for them.

However, we *did* set up a new spiritual vibration through our ascent to Oz that just might resonate with them, enticing them to begin their very own sacred path, if they so choose.

Now that we've walked down *The Yellow Brick Road*, we have changed. They control us, and we feel their concern. They discourage us from being different, and we feel their love. What was, prior to our whirlwind, a wretchedly, restrictive, painful human life on the farm, has been converted. Through the *Oz State of Mind*, it's been transformed into a perfect expression of Grace. It's now a Divine Message that speaks to our Mind, Heart, and Will, simultaneously, the *Still Small Voice* within us. We now know every bad witch is a good witch in disguise; we've removed the disguise and can see the Light of God in all. We now own our broomstick. Our pain is melting… melting.

Home is that place within each and every one of us, where we know that the Perfection of God's Love is alive and breathing through the ordinariness of our fleshly lives. Yes, the simple ordinariness of everyday life! That's where God lives!

Home is the certain knowledge of inward-faith, of there being a God that is Good, and that God's Presence is equally within each of us, regardless of our earthly circumstances, fortunate or not.

Therefore, Life is filled with hope, with optimism, with God's Own Promise.

*"Oh, Auntie Em. There's no place like home!,"* Dorothy chimes, as the huge orchestral crescendo ends the movie.

That's a prayer all of us should say upon waking in our bed each morning, after the cyclone of our dreams or nightmares has descended back to earth. That's the only prayer there is:

**"There's no place like home!"**

Michael Shevack has taught Spirituality and Comparative Religion in the School of Social Welfare at the State University of New York (Stony Brook). He has lectured in Business Spirituality at the Iacocca Institute for Global Entrepreneurship at Lehigh University, and Shippensburg University. Actively engaged in inter-religious dialogue around the world, he is the author of six books, and is a consultant to numerous organizations and businesses.

He is married to artist Teddy Frank and has three children: Christian, Adam and Zoe.

CPSIA information can be obtained
at www.ICGtesting.com
Printed in the USA
LVHW051453030121
675568LV00021B/3499